FORREST GUMP

영화읽기

이향만 영문학 박사, 호서대학교 영어영문학과 교수

저서: 『영화로 읽는 미국소설』 1~5권
　　　1권: 『톰소여와 헉핀의 모험』 / 2권: 『분노의 포도』 / 3권: 『생쥐와 인간』 / 4권: 『위대한 개츠비』 / 5권: 『주홍글자』
　　　『미국소설과 영화의 만남』

주요 논문
　　　"현대인의 성과 자유" – 존 업다이크와 필립 로스 소설연구(박사학위논문)
　　　"다원사회에서의 인디언 정신 – 루이스 어드릭의 『사랑의 묘약』"
　　　"필립 로스의 카운터라이프 – 자아변형의 미학"
　　　"필립 로스의 '미국소설 쓰기'"
　　　"필립 로스의 〈주커만 연작소설〉"
　　　"닫힌 세계와 열린 의식 – 조이스 캐롤 오츠의 소설"
　　　"더불어 서기의 새로운 의미 – 바바라 킹솔버의 소설"

발행일 • 2008년 2월 25일
편저자 • 이향만/ 발행인 • 이성모 / 발행처 • 도서출판 동인
서울시 종로구 명륜동 2가 237 아남주상복합④ 118호/ 등록 • 제1-1599호
TEL • (02) 765-7145/ FAX • (02) 765-7165/ E-mail • dongin60@chollian.net/ Homepage • donginbook.co.kr

ISBN 978-89-5506-352-3 13740   정가 10,000원

FORREST GUMP 영화 읽기

이향만 편저

도서출판 동인

CONTENTS

EPISODE 1. Life Is Like a Box of Chocolate 7

EPISODE 2. Stupid is as Stupid Does! 25

EPISODE 3. The Answer Is Blowing In the Wind 47

EPISODE 4. We all Have a Destiny 69

EPISODE 5. A Promise Is a Promise 91

EPISODE 6. Do the Best with What God Gave You 113

EPISODE 7. Put the Past Behind You! 131

EPISODE 8. I Pronounce You Man and Wife 151

EPISODE 9. Dying Is a Part of Life 167

APPENDIX The Commencement Address 181
— by Steve Jobs

Episode 1

Life Is Like a Box of Chocolate

A Man and His Shoes

SITUATIONs 1

Warming-up Questions & Listening Practice

1. *How much does Forrest like his chocolate?*

   Hello. My name's Forrest Gump. You want a chocolate?
   I could eat about a million and a half of these.

2. *What did Momma say about life?*
   Why do you think she said so?

   My mother always said, "Life was like a box of chocolates.
   You never know what you're gonna get."

3. *What does Forrest say about the black woman's shoes?*
   And how did the lady respond to Forrest?

   "Those must be comfortable shoes.
   I'll bet you could walk all day in shoes like that and not feel a thing.

I wish I had shoes like that."

"My feet hurt."

4. *According to Momma, what can we tell about a person by their shoes?*

   Momma always says there's an awful lot you could tell about a person by their shoes, where they're going, where they've been.

5. *What is Forrest going to tell the lady about?*

   I've worn lots of shoes. I bet if I think about it real hard I could remember my first pair of shoes. Momma said they'd take me anywhere.

Listen to the audio and check!

FORREST: Hello. My name's Forrest Gump. You want a chocolate? I could eat about a million and a half of these.[1] My momma always said, "Life was[is] like a box of chocolates. You never know what you're gonna get."
[*looks down at the nurse's shoes.*] Those must be comfortable shoes. I'll bet you could walk all day in shoes like that and not feel a thing. I wish I had shoes like that.

WOMAN: My feet hurt.
FORREST: Momma always says there's an awful lot you could tell about a person by their shoes, where they're going, where

1) 백만 개 이상도 먹을 수 있을 겁니다. (초코렛이 있기만 하다면)

they've been. [*The black woman stares at Forrest as he looks down at his own shoes.*] I've worn lots of shoes. I bet if I think about it real hard I could remember my first pair of shoes. Momma said they'd take me anywhere.

TOPICs to DISCUSS
Read the following review and develop your own idea.

> The first thing we see in *Forrest Gump* is a single white feather, floating against the blue sky, drifting in the breeze as it floats over Savannah, Ga., and eventually settles at the feet of a man sitting on a bus bench.
>
> The feather is symbolic, of course, and as the film progresses we see that the title character, that man on the bench, is an innocent who has been tossed about by the winds of change in America, spanning the turbulent decades of the '50s, '60s and '70s. Yet, through it all, he has remained ever optimistic.
>
> – By Chris Hicks

… **A** Discuss the philosophy of life which is represented in Momma's saying, "Life is a box of chocolate."

… **B** As Forrest Gump begins, we see a white feather floating against a blue sky.
Think about the thematic implication of a white feather.

Episode 1. Life Is Like a Box of Chocolate

Forrest and His Magic Shoes

SITUATIONs 2

Warming-up Questions & Listening Practice

1. *What did Forrest wear?*

   She said they was[were] my magic shoes.

2. *Why did Forrest wear his magic shoes?*

   But his back is as crooked as a politician.
   But we're gonna straighten him right up now, won't we, Forrest?

3. *What is Forrest's back like?*

   His legs are strong, Mrs. Gump, as strong as I've ever seen.
   But his back is as crooked as a politician.

4. *How does the doctor cure Forrest's crooked back?*

   But we're gonna straighten him right up now, won't we, Forrest?

5. *How is Forrest named?*

   Now, when I was a baby, Momma named me after the great Civil War hero, General Nathan Bedford Forrest.

6. *Why is Forrest named after General Forrest?*

   She said we was[were] related to him in some way.
   And anyway, that's how I got my name. Forrest Gump.

7. *What is General Forrest notorious for?*
   Was Forrest's mother proud of her son's name?

   What he did was, he started up this club called the Ku Klux Klan.

8. *How did the people of the K.K.K look like?*

   They'd all dress up in their robes and their bed sheets and act like a bunch of ghosts or spooks or something. They'd even put bed sheets on their horses and ride around.

9. *How did Mother evaluate making the name of the Forrest part?*

   Momma said that the Forrest part was to remind me that sometimes we all do things that, well, just don't make no sense.

Listen to the audio and check!

[*Forrest sits in a doctor's office.*]

FORREST(V.O.)   She said they was my magic shoes. [*Forrest has been fitted with orthopedic shoes and metal leg braces.*]

DOCTOR: All right, Forrest, you can open your eyes now. Let's take a little walk around. [*The doctor sets Forrest down on its feet. Forrest walks around stiffly.*]
[*to Forrest*] How do those feel?
[*to Forrest's mother*] His legs are strong, Mrs. Gump, as strong as I've ever seen. But his back is as crooked as a politician.[2] But we're gonna straighten him right up now, won't we, Forrest?

Mrs. Gump and young Forrest walk across the street. Forrest walks stiffly next to his mother.

FORREST(V.O.)   Now, when I was a baby, Momma named me after the great Civil War hero [3], General Nathan Bedford Forrest. She said we was related to him in some way. [4] What he did

---

2) 정치가들이 양식이 뒤틀리고 닳아빠진 현상에 빗대어 주인공의 등이 구부러져 있다고 말하고 있음.
   * "Crooked" can mean marked by bends or curves, but it also means corrupt and dishonest.
3) 남북전쟁 때의 위대한 영웅의 이름을 따라 지었다.
4) 먼 친척 같은 관계이다.

was, he started up this club called the Ku Klux Klan.5) They'd all dress up in their robes and their bed sheets and act like a bunch of ghosts or spooks or something.6)

They'd even put bed sheets on their horses and ride around. And anyway, that's how I got my name. Forrest Gump. Momma said that the Forrest part was to remind me that sometimes we all do things that, well, just don't make no sense.

[Mrs. Gump and Forrest walk along the sidewalk past the two old men. Mrs. Gump holds tightly onto Forrest's hand.]

TOPICs to DISCUSS

… A   Discuss the theme that is represented by Doctor's saying about crookedness of Forrest and a politician.

… B   What can you infer by the story of General Nathan Bedford and Forrest Gump?

---

5) KKK단이라고 불리는 단체. 1860년대부터 흑인들에 대한 폭력으로 악명 높았던 백인 인종차별주의자 단체.
6) 침대 덮개 같은 하얀 천으로 복장을 하고 마치 유령처럼 행동하다. * A Spook: 유령(a ghost.)

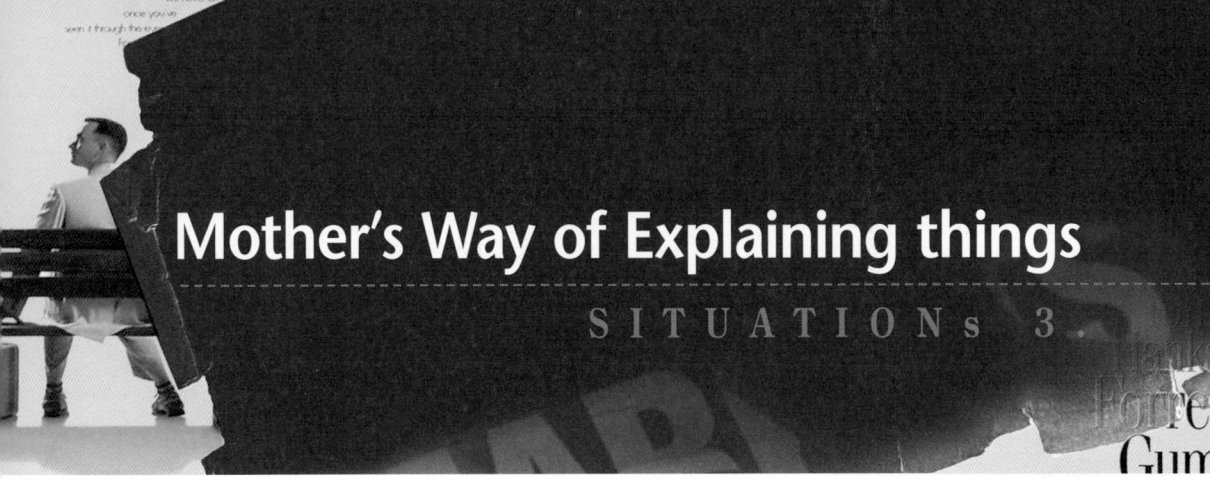

Mother's Way of Explaining things

SITUATIONs 3.

Warming-up Questions & Listening Practice

1. *How does Mother respond to people who watch Forrest?*

   What are you all staring at? Haven't you ever seen a little boy with braces on his legs before?

2. *How does Mother advise Forrest to overcome the inferiority complex?*

   Don't ever let anybody tell you they're better than you, Forrest.

3. *How does Mother explain God's will about Forrest's brace on his legs?*

   If God intended everybody to be the same, he'd have given us all braces on our legs.

4. *How does Mother always explain all things to Forrest?*

   Momma always had a way of explaining things so I could understand them.

5. *Where is Forrest's house located?*

   We lived about a quarter mile of Route 17, about a half mile from the town of Greenbow, Alabama. That's in the county of Greenbow.

6. *Is Forrest's house in Momma's family or Father's family?*

   Our house had been in Momma's family since her grandpa's, grandpa's grandpa had come across the ocean about a thousand years ago. Something like that.

7. *Why did Forrest and his mother have all the empty rooms?*

   Since it was just me and Momma and we had all these empty rooms,

8. *Why did Mother decide to let those rooms out? And for what?*

   Momma decided to let those rooms out, mostly to people passing through, like from, oh, Mobile, Montgomery, place like that.
   That's how me and Mommy got money. Mommy was a real smart lady.

9. *What is the advice about life that Mother wants her son to remember?*

   Remember what I told you, Forrest. You're no different than anybody else is. Did you hear what I said, Forrest? You're the same as everybody else. You are no different.

Listen to the audio and check!

MRS. GUMP: Just wait, let me get it. Let me get it. Wait, get it this way. Hold on. Oooh. All right.
[*to the men on the street*]
What are you all staring at? Haven't you ever seen a little boy with braces on his legs before?

MRS. GUMP: [*to Forrest*] Don't ever let anybody tell you they're better than you, Forrest.
If God intended everybody to be the same, he'd have given us all braces on our legs.

FORREST(V.O.): Momma always had a way of explaining things so I could understand them.

FORREST(V.O.): We lived about a quarter mile of Route 17, about a half mile from the town of Greenbow, Alabama. That's in the county of Greenbow. Our house had been in Momma's family since her grandpa's, grandpa's grandpa 7) had come across the ocean about a thousand years ago. Something like that. Since it was just me and Momma and we had all these

7) 외가쪽 오래된 할아버지 조상을 가리키는 표현.

empty rooms, Momma decided to let those rooms out, [8] mostly to people passing through, like from, oh, Mobile, Montgomery, place like that. That's how me and Mommy got money. Mommy was a real smart lady.

MRS. GUMP: Remember what I told you, Forrest. You're no different than anybody else is. Did you hear what I said, Forrest? You're the same as everybody else. You are no different.

TOPICs to DISCUSS

> Discuss theme of difference and discrimination represented in the above story.

8) 방을 세놓다. "rent out."

Episode 1. Life Is Like a Box of Chocolate

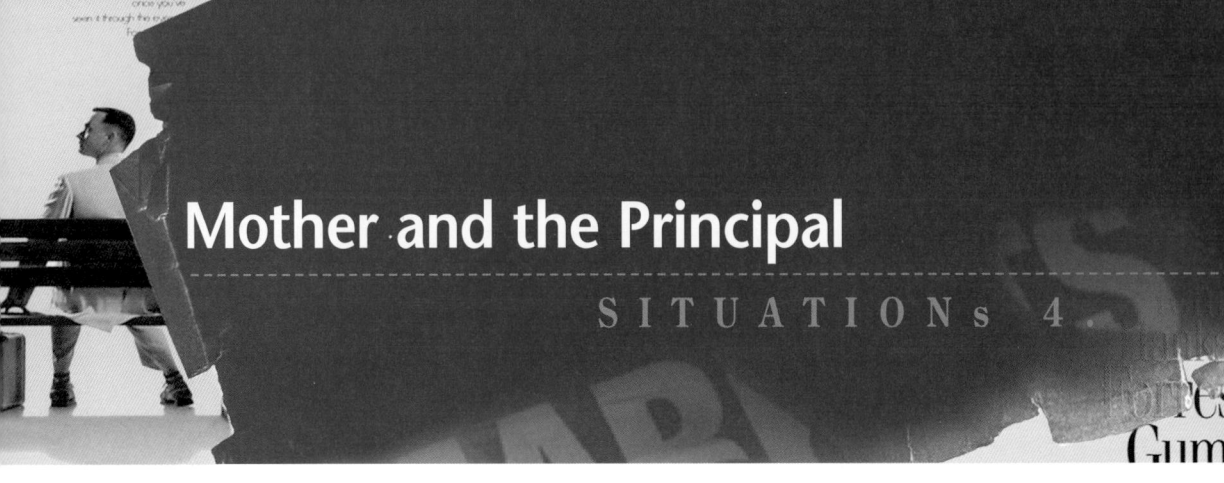

Mother and the Principal
SITUATIONs 4

Warming-up Questions & Listening Practice

1. *Why does the principal think is Forrest different?*
   And how does Momma reply to him?

   "Your boy's different, Mrs. Gump. Now, his I.Q. is seventy-five."
   "Well, we're all different, Mr. Hancock."

2. *Why did Mother Forrest come to meet the principal?*

   She wanted me to have the finest education, so she took me to the Greenbow County Central School. I met the principal and all.

3. *What is required of the student to attend a public school?*

   "I want to show you something, Mrs. Gump. Now, this is normal. Forrest is right here. The State requires a minimum I.Q. of eighty to attend a public school, Mrs. Gump."

4. *What does Momma think of Forrest's intelligence?*

   "What does normal mean, anyway? He might be a bit on the slow side, but my boy Forrest is going to get the same opportunities as everyone else."

5. *Why doesn't Mother want Forrest to go to a special school?*

   "He's not going to some special school to learn to how to re-tread tires. We're talking about five little points here. There must be something can be done."

6. *What is the principal worried about Forrest's coming to his school?*

   "We're a progressive school system. We don't want to see anybody left behind."

7. *Why did Momma say, "He's on vacation." And what does it mean?*

   "Is there a Mr. Gump, Mrs. Gump?"
   "He's on vacation."

Listen to the audio and check!

INT. ELEMENTARY SCHOOL/ PRINCIPAL'S OFFICE–DAY

PRINCIPAL: Your boy's different, Mrs. Gump. Now, his I.Q. is seventy-five. 9)

MRS. GUMP: Well, we're all different, Mr. Hancock.

[*Forrest sits outside the principal's office and waits.*]

FORREST(V.O.): She wanted me to have the finest education, so she took me to the Greenbow County Central School. I met the principal and all.

[*The principal stands in front of Mrs. Gump. Forrest, sitting left, listens.*]

PRINCIPAL: I want to show you something, Mrs. Gump. Now, this is normal. Forrest is right here. The State requires a minimum I.Q. of eighty to attend public school, Mrs. Gump. He's gonna have to go to a special school. Now, he'll be just fine.

MRS. GUMP: What does normal mean, anyway? He might be a bit on the slow side, 10) but my boy Forrest is going to get the same

---

9) 댁의 아들은 다릅니다. 그의 지능지수가 75밖에 되지 않습니다.
10) 그 애는 지능이 조금 늦게 깨는 편입니다.

opportunities as everyone else. He's not going to some special school to learn to how to re-tread tires. [11] **We're talking about five little points here. There must be something can be done.**

PRINCIPAL: We're a progressive school system. We don't want to see anybody left behind. Is there a Mr. Gump, Mrs. Gump?

MRS. GUMP: He's on vacation.

TOPICs to DISCUSS

Read the following review and develop your own idea.

> There is a long and fascinating tradition of the holy fool in spiritual literature. These people follow the dictates of the heart and are often able to effect great works of mercy and compassion. Their brand of selflessness is free of reason's

---

11) 그 애를 타이어 입히는 일이나 시키기 위해 특수학교에는 절대 보내지 않을 겁니다.

madness and the ego's frivolous grandeur. Holy fools pay no heed to the worldly pursuit of power, status, or financial success. That is why they are usually deemed crazy and forced to live as lonely outsiders. Forrest Gump is an enchanting and creative parable about a contemporary holy fool.

– By Frederic and Mary Ann Brussat

... **A** Compare the values of education between Momma and the principal.
... **B** Discuss Momma's passion for her son's education.

Episode 2

Stupid is as Stupid Does!

Forrest and Jenny

SITUATIONs 1.

Warming-up Questions & Listening Practice

1. *What does Forrest think is funny?*

   It's funny how you remember some things,

2. *What does Forrest remember very well?*

   I remember the bus ride on the first day of school very well.

3. *Why does Forrest hesitate to take a ride on the bus?*

   Momma said not to be taking rides from strangers.

4. *When does Forrest begin to get on the school bus?*

   This is the bus to school. We ain't strangers anymore.

Listen to the audio and check!

FORREST(V.O.): You know, it's funny how you remember some things, but some things you can't.
MRS. GUMP: You do your very best now, Forrest.
FORREST: I sure will, Momma.
FORREST(V.O.): I remember the bus ride on the first day of school very well. [*The bus driver opens the door and looks down.*]

BUS DRIVER: Are you comin' along?
FORREST: Momma said not to be taking rides from strangers.[1]
BUS DRIVER: This is the bus to school.

1) Mama said to not to be taking rides from strangers: 어머니는 낯선 사람의 차를 타지 말라고 했습니다.

Episode 2. Stupid is as Stupid Does!

FORREST:	I'm Forrest Gump.
BUS DRIVER:	I'm Dorothy Harris.
FORREST:	Well, now we ain't strangers anymore. [*Forrest steps up onto the bus.*]

TOPICs to DISCUSS

Most people agree that Forrest Gump is a very simple-minded person, nevertheless, he often sees things in their correct perspective trotting out pearls of wisdom.

In your groups, make a list of words and phrases that best describe Forrest's character.

Forrest on the School bus

SITUATIONs 2.

Warming-up Questions & Listening Practice

1. *What does the children say to Gump?*

   This seat's taken. / You can't sit here.
   (Is this seat taken?/ May I sit here?)
   You can sit here if you want.

2. *What does Forrest think is funny?*

   You know, it's funny what a young man recollects, 'cause I don't remember being born. I, I… don't recall what I got for my first Christmas and I don't know when I went on my first outdoor picnic.

3. *What is it that Forrest remembers very well?*

   But, I do remember the first time I heard the sweetest voice in the wide world.

Episode 2. Stupid is as Stupid Does!

4. **What was the most beautiful Forrest had ever seen?**

   I had never seen anything so beautiful in my life.
   She was like an angel.

5. **About what was Jenny wondering?**

   "What's wrong with your legs?"
   "Um, nothing at all, thank you. My legs are just fine and dandy."

6. **How did Forrest explain to Jenny about his shoes?**

   Then why do you have those shoes on?
   My momma said my back's crooked like a question mark. These are going to make me as straight as an arrow. They're my magic shoes.

7. **What did Forrest say about being stupid?**

   Mommy says stupid is as stupid does.

Listen to the audio and check!

BOY #1: This seat's taken.
BOY #2: It's taken!
BOY #3: You can't sit here.
FORREST(V.O.): You know, it's funny what a young man recollects, 'cause I don't remember being born. I, I… don't recall what I got for my first Christmas and I don't know when I went on my first outdoor picnic. But, I do remember the first time I heard the sweetest voice in the wide world.

[Forrest looks back at a young girl about Forrest's age.]
GIRL: You can sit here if you want.
FORREST(V.O.): I had never seen anything so beautiful in my life. She was

Episode 2. Stupid is as Stupid Does!

	like an angel.
JENNY:	Well, are you gonna sit down, or aren't ya?
	[*Forrest sits down next to Jenny.*]
	What's wrong with your legs?
FORREST:	Um, nothing at all, thank you. My legs are just fine and dandy. 2)
FORREST(V.O.):	I just sat next to her on that bus and had conversation all the way to school.
JENNY:	Then why do you have those shoes on?
FORREST:	My momma said my back's crooked like a question mark. 3) These are going to make me as straight as an arrow. 4) They're my magic shoes.
FORREST(V.O.):	And next to Momma, no one ever talked to me or asked me questions.
JENNY:	Are you stupid or something?
FORREST:	Mommy says stupid is as stupid does. 5)
	Jenny puts her hand out toward Forrest. Forrest reaches over and shakes her hand.
JENNY:	I'm Jenny.
FORREST:	I'm Forrest Gump. Forrest Gump.

2) My legs are just fine and dandy: A curious and somewhat old-fashioned expression meaning good, or well.
3) 의문부호 "?"처럼 (허리가) 구부러져 있다.
4) 화살처럼 반듯하다.
5) 바보는 외모 때문에 바보인 것이 아니고 하는 행위 때문에 바보인 것이다. 이 영화 때문에 유명해진 말.
("Just because you look stupid, you're not stupid unless you do stupid things.")

TOPICs to DISCUSS

One of the big issues in the film is discrimination against those who are different from others in some way. Is it true? How do we act towards those who are different from us (less intelligent, handicapped, sick, racially different, different skin colour, a different religion. Do we respect them? Do we ignore them? Do we make fun of them? Do we reject them? Why? Why not?

Like Peas and Carrots

SITUATIONs 3

WATCH the MOVIE

Warming-up Questions & Listening Practice

1. *How does Forrest describe his friendship with Jenny?*

   From that day on, we was[were] always together.
   Jenny and me was[were] like peas and carrots.

2. *What did Jenny teach Forrest to do?*
   And what did Forrest show Jenny to do?

   She taught me how to climb. I showed her how to dangle. She helped me to learn how to read. And I showed her to swing. Sometimes we'd just sit out and wait for the stars.

3. *Forrest's Momma always told that miracles happen every day.*
   What is it about Forrest Gump?

   Now, my Momma always told me that miracles happen every day.

Some people don't think so, but they do.

4. *What happened that helped Forrest learn to run?*

Now, you wouldn't believe it if I told you. But I can run like the wind blows. From that day on, if I was going somewhere, I was running!

Listen to the audio and check!

FORREST(V.O.): From that day on, we was always together. Jenny and me was like peas and carrots. 6) She taught me how to climb. I showed her how to dangle. She helped me to learn how to read. And I showed her to swing. Sometimes we'd just sit out and wait for the stars.
FORREST: Momma's gonna worry about me.
JENNY: Just stay a little longer.
FORREST(V.O.): For some reason, Jenny didn't never want to go home.
FORREST: Okay, Jenny. I'll stay.
FORREST(V.O.): She was my most special friend. My only friend.

6) We was like peas and carrots: 바늘과 실처럼 항상 함께 했다.
   ("we went together well, and became best friends,")

[*Forrest continues talking to the black woman.*]

FORREST(V.O.): Now, my Momma always told me that miracles happen every day. Some people don't think so, but they do.
Now, you wouldn't believe it if I told you. But I can run like the wind blows. From that day on, if I was going somewhere, I was running!

TOPICs to DISCUSS

Read the following review and develop your own idea.

> The movie's seeming connection between low intelligence and innocence would be unsettling if it weren't for Hanks' ability to suggest that Forrest's goodness comes from someplace deep inside his heart that is in no way connected to his ability to understand complex phenomena. The movie makes it clear that Forrest never fully comprehends everything that happens around him, yet that has little bearing on how he treats the people he loves.
>
> Describe how running helped Forrest throughout his life.

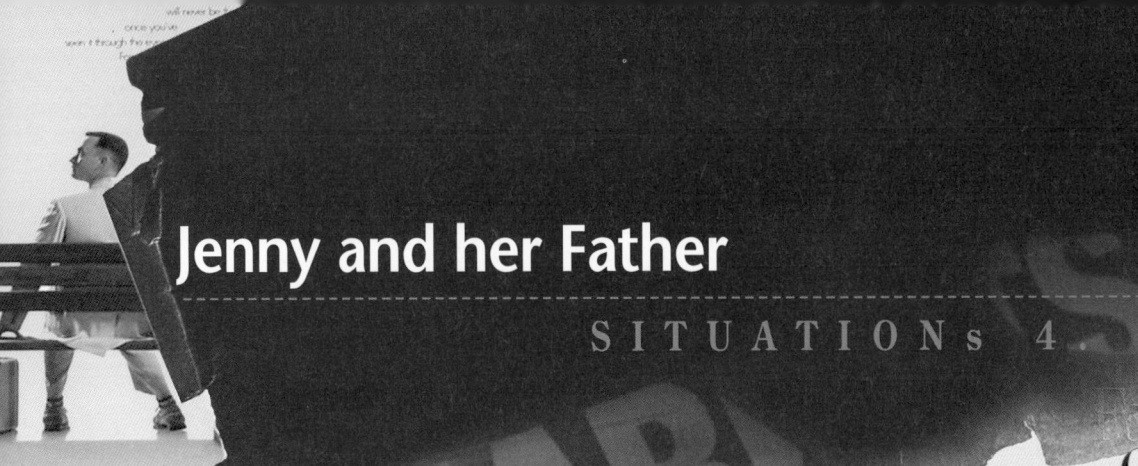

Jenny and her Father

SITUATIONs 4

Warming-up Questions & Listening Practice

1. *Where did Jenny live?*

   Well, she lived in a house that was as old as Alabama.

2. *When did Jenny's mother die?*

   Her Momma had gone up to heaven when she was five.

3. *What was the job of Jenny's father?*

   Her Momma had gone up to heaven when she was five and her daddy was some kind of a farmer.

4. *Why didn't Jenny come to school today?*

   He was a very lovin' man. He was always kissing and touchin' her and her sisters. And then this one time, Jenny wasn't on the bus to go to school.

5. *What did Jenny pray for?*

Pray with me. Dear God, make me a bird so I can fly far, far, far away from here.

Listen to the audio and check!

FORREST(V.O.): Now remember how I told you that Jenny never seemed to want to go home? Well, she lived in a house that was as old as Alabama. Her Momma had gone up to heaven when she was five [7] and her daddy was some kind of a farmer.

Forrest knocks on Jenny's door.

FORREST: Jenny? Jenny? [*Forrest look around the field at the left. He notices Jenny and runs toward her.*]

FORREST(V.O.): He was a very lovin' man. He was always kissing and touchin' her and her sisters. And then this one time, Jenny wasn't on the bus to go to school. [*Forrest runs to Jenny.*]

FORREST: Jenny, why didn't you come to school today?

JENNY: Hsh! Daddy's takin' a nap. [*Jenny grabs Forrest's hand and runs into the field. Jenny's DAD drunk, steps out onto the porch and shouts.*]

JENNY'S DAD: Jenny!

JENNY: Come on!

JENNY'S DAD: Jenny, where'd you run to? You'd better come back here, girl! Where you at? Jenny! Jenny! Where you at? Jenny!

7) 다섯 살 때 어머니가 세상을 떠났다.

[*Jenny drops to her knees and pulls Forrest down with her.*]

JENNY: Pray with me, Forrest. Pray with me. Dear God, make me a bird so I can fly far, far, far away from here. Dear God, make me a bird so I can fly far, far, far away from here.

TOPICs to DISCUSS

Read the following review and develop your own idea.

Counterbalancing the rather saccharine story of Forrest are the tragic stories of Jenny (Robin Wright) and Lieutenant Dan (Gary Sinise). While Forrest stays pretty much in the American mainstream, Jenny takes a prolonged tour of the counterculture, from being a free-spirited hippie to snorting cocaine in a 1970s disco. Lieutenant Dan has his legs blown off in the Vietnam War, leaving him with a bitterness that Forrest later helps him work through. But the film does manage to strike just the right note of poignancy when Lieutenant Dan comes to see Forrest and Jenny get married in 1981, apparently symbolizing the reconciliation of various segments of American society that had become estranged during the turbulence of the 1960s and 1970s.

Jenny's New House

SITUATIONs 5.

Warming-up Questions & Listening Practice

1. *Why did Forrest introduce Momma's words that God is mysterious? What is God's answer to Jenny's prayer?*

   He didn't turn Jenny into a bird that day. Instead he had the police say Jenny didn't have to stay in that house no more.

2. *Where did Jenny go to live instead of her father's house?*

   She went to live with her grandma just over on Creekmore Avenue, which made me happy 'cause she was so close.

3. *At night, why did Jenny sneak out and come over to Forrest's house?*

   Some nights, Jenny'd sneak out and come over to my house, just 'cause she said she was scared.

4. *What did Forrest think was Jenny scare of?*

   Scared of what, I don't know but I think it was her grandma's dog. He was a mean dog.

5. *Until when were Jenny and Forrest best friends?*

   Anyway, Jenny and me was best friends all the way to high school.

Listen to the audio and check!

FORREST(V.O.): Momma always said that God is mysterious. He didn't turn Jenny into a bird that day.
Instead, he had the police say Jenny didn't have to stay in that house no more. She was to live with her grandma just over on Creekmore Avenue, which made me happy 'cause she was so close.
Some nights, Jenny'd sneak out and come over to my house, just 'cause she said she was scared. Scared of what, I don't know. But I think it was her grandma's dog. He was a mean dog.
Anyway, Jenny and me was best friends all the way up through high school.

TOPICs to DISCUSS

Read the following review and develop your own idea.

> The love of Forrest's life, Jenny (Robin Wright), is more troubled. Abused by her father as a child, she seems to be in constant torment, latching on to political movements and anarchic lifestyles until she eventually figures out how to make peace with herself.
>
> – *by Chris Hicks*

Episode 3

The Answer Is Blowing In the Wind

Forrest and Kennedy

SITUATIONs 1

Warming-up Questions & Listening Practice

1. *How did Forrest spend his college life?*

   College ran by real fast 'cause I played so much football.

2. *Why did Forrest have the pleasure to meet the President of the United States?*

   They even put me on a thing called the All-America Team where you get to meet the President of the United States.

3. *According to the news, where did the president meet the football players?*

   President Kennedy met with the Collegiate All-American Football Team at the Oval Office today.

4. *What is the real good thing about meeting the President of the United States?*

   Now, the real good thing about meeting the President of the United States is the food.
   They put you in this little room with just about anything you'd want to eat or drink.

5. *Why did Forrest drink so much Dr. Peppers?*

   And since number one, I wasn't hungry, but thirsty, and number two, they was free, I musta drank me about fifteen Dr. Peppers.

6. *What question did the President ask the members of the American Team?*

   Congratulations. How does it feel to be an All-American?

7. *What did Forrest say when the President ask a question?*

   Congratulations. How do you feel?
   I gotta pee.
   I believe he said he had to go pee.

8. *Where did Kennedy get shot and why?*

   Sometime later, for no particular reason, somebody shot that nice young President when he was ridin' in his car.

Episode 3. The Answer Is Blowing In the Wind

9. *Where did Kennedy's younger brother get shot?*

And a few years after that somebody shot his little brother, too, only he was in a hotel kitchen.

Listen to the audio and check!

[*WHITE HOUSE RECEPTION AREA: The All-American players mingle around the food table.*]

FORREST(V.O.): College ran by real fast 'cause I played so much football. They even put me on a thing called the All-America Team where you get to meet the President of the United States.

ANNOUNCER: [*over newsreel*] President Kennedy met with the Collegiate All-American[1] Football Team at the Oval Office today.[2]

FORREST(V.O.): Now, the real good thing about meeting the President of the United States is the food.
They put you in this little room with just about anything you'd want to eat or drink. And since number one, I wasn't hungry, but thirsty, and number two, they was free, I musta drank me about fifteen Dr. Peppers.

President Kennedy shakes hands with the All-American football players.

PRESIDENT: Congratulations. How does it feel to be an All-American?

1ST PLAYER: It's an honor, Sir. [*Another player steps up to the President and shakes the*

1) 전미 우수 미식축구 선수 팀
2) 미국 대통령 집무실

	President's hand.]
PRESIDENT:	Congratulations. How does it feel to be an All-American?
2ND PLAYER:	Very good, Sir.
PRESIDENT:	Congratulations. How does it feel to be an All-American?
3RD PLAYER:	Very good, Sir.

[*The President shakes Forrest's hand and asks.*]

PRESIDENT:	Congratulations. How do you feel?
FORREST:	I gotta pee. President Kennedy turns and smiles.
PRESIDENT:	I believe he said he had to go pee.

[*Forrest urinates in the bathroom, and then notices photo of Marilyn Monroe.*]

FORREST(V.O.): Sometime later, for no particular reason, somebody shot that nice young President when he was ridin' in his car. And a few years after that somebody shot his little brother, too, only he was in a hotel kitchen. It must be hard being brothers. I wouldn't know.

TOPICs to DISCUSS

Read the following review and develop your own idea.

FORREST GUMP was often criticised for its revisionist version of modern American history and less than flattering portrayal of individuals and movements that tried to change status quo of American society. Protagonist, instead of trying to change the world, simply follows the rules, obeys his parents and authorities and gets his reward in the form of business success and family happiness. On the other hand, those who try to rebel and be smarter than the average masses are those who are going to be punished with violence, drugs, AIDS and disillusionment. Some might find traces of Taoism in philosophy of *FORREST GUMP*, but in the end Groom, Roth and Zemeckis provide ending closer to Hegelian dialectics– Gump, as embodiment of "proper" America, and Jenny, as embodiment of counter–culture– reconcile their differences in bittersweet ending that gives hope for future generations. However, many viewers would care little about philosophy or political views displayed in this film; what they would really appreciate is the quality of filmmaking and the way it was used for the purposes of good, human, uplifting story–something we rarely see in Hollywood these days.

Shrimping Boat

SITUATIONs 2.

Warming-up Questions & Listening Practice

1. *How did Gump feel on his induction day?*

    At first, it seemed like I made a mistake, seeing how it was my induction day and I was already gettin' yelled at.

2. *What kindness did Bubba offer to Forrest?*

    You can sit down if you want to. I didn't know who I might meet or what they might ask.

3. *What question did Bubba ask Forrest?*

    You ever been on a real shrimp boat?
    No, but I been on a real big boat.
    I'm talkin' about a shrimp catchin' boat.

Forrest Gump 영화읽기

4. *Explain about Bubba's experience in shrimping business.*

   I've been workin' on shrimp boats all my life. I started out my uncle's boat, that's my mother's brother, when I was about maybe nine.

5. *Explain about the history of Bubba's name.*

   My given name is Benjamin Buford Blue. People call me Bubba, just like one of them redneck boys. Can you believe that?

6. *What is Bubba's dream?*

   I was just lookin' into buyin' a boat of my own and got drafted.

7. *Where is Bubba come from and what did his family do for a living?*

   So Bubba was from Bayou La Batre, Alabama, and his momma cooked shrimp. And her momma before her cooked shrimp. And her momma before her momma cooked shrimp, too.

8. *About what do Bubba's family know everything?*

   Bubba's family knew everything there was to know about the shrimpin' business.

Listen to the audio and check!

Forrest steps forward, looking much like he did on his first bus ride to school years ago. A large black recruit with a strange look on his face, much like Forrest's, looks up from his seat. His name is BUBBA.

FORREST(V.O.):	At first, it seemed like I made a mistake, seeing how it was my induction day 3) and I was already gettin' yelled at. 4)
BUBBA:	You can sit down if you want to.
FORREST(V.O.):	I didn't know who I might meet or what they might ask.
	[*Bubba hands Forrest a handkerchief.*]
BUBBA:	You ever been on a real shrimp boat?
FORREST:	No, but I been on a real big boat.
BUBBA:	I'm talkin' about a shrimp catchin' boat. I've been workin' on shrimp boats all my life. I started out my uncle's boat, that's my mother's brother, when I was about maybe nine. I was just lookin' into buyin' a boat of my own and got drafted. 5)

---

3) 입대 첫날
4) I was already getting yelled at: 고함을 치는 소리를 들었다.
5) I was looking to buy a boat on my own and then I got drafted: 내 명의의 배를 사고 싶어 입대했다.

	My given name is Benjamin Buford Blue. People call me Bubba, just like one of them redneck boys.⁶⁾ Can you believe that?
FORREST:	My name's Forrest Gump. People call me Forrest Gump.
FORREST(V.O.):	So Bubba was from Bayou La Batre, Alabama, and his momma cooked shrimp. And her momma before her cooked shrimp. And her momma before her momma cooked shrimp, too. Bubba's family knew everything there was to know about the shrimpin' business.
BUBBA:	I know everything there is to know about the shrimpin' business. Matter of fact, I'm goin' into the shrimpin' business for myself after I get out the Army.
FORREST:	Okay.

TOPICs to DISCUSS

Read the following review and develop your own idea.

> Jenny and Forrest both start out in the same place. Forrest works hard without questioning anything, sure he gets some tough breaks but his dogged efforts eventually work out for him. Jenny, on the other hand, gets involved in the other culture of the times be it political rebellion, drugs, music, extramarital sex etc.

6) 못 배우고 교양이 없는 집안 출신의 아이들을 가리키는 속어.

Episode 3. The Answer Is Blowing In the Wind

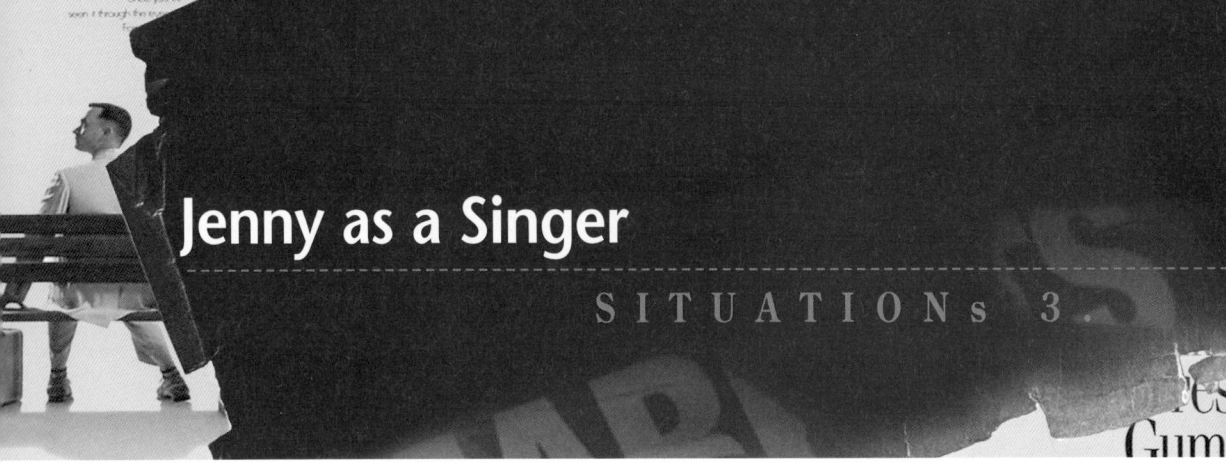

Jenny as a Singer

SITUATIONs 3.

Warming-up Questions & Listening Practice

1. *Why was Jenny thrown out of school?*

   Turns out, Jenny had gotten into some trouble over some photos of her in her college sweater.

2. *Why wasn't it a bad thing for Jenny to get into some trouble because of her photos?*

   Because a man who owns a theater in Memphis, Tennessee, saw those photo and offered Jenny a job singing in a show.

3. *Why did Forrest take the bus up to Memphis?*

   The first chance I got, I took the bus up to Memphis to see her perform in that show.

Forrest Gump 영화읽기

4. *How did the MC introduce Jenny to the audience?*

   Give her a big hand, guys!
   Good job, Amber. And now, for your listening and viewing pleasure, direct from Hollywood, California, our very own beatnik beauty, let's give a big round of applause to the luscious Bobbie Dylan.

5. *What song did Jenny sing?*

   "The answer, my friend is blowing in the wind. The answer is blowing in!"

6. *In the song, where does the white dove sleep?*

   "Yes, and how many seas must the white dove sail, before she sleeps in the sand?"

7. *Why did Forrest think Jenny's dream had come true?*

   Her dream had come true. She was a folk singer.

8. *How many times must the cannonballs fly before they're forever banned?*

   "Yes, how many times must the cannonballs fly before they're forever banned." "The answer, my friend is blowing in the wind."

Episode 3.   The Answer Is Blowing In the Wind

Listen to the audio and check!

Forrest pick up the magazine and turns the page, revealing Jenny as she poses with a school sweater on, and that's all. The pictorial is titled: "Girls of the South."

FORREST(V.O.): Turns out, Jenny had gotten into some trouble over some photos of her in her college sweater. And she was thrown out of school.

[*At the Nashville night club*]

But that wasn't a bad thing. Because a man who owns a theater in Memphis, Tennessee, saw those photo and offered Jenny a job singing in a show. The first chance I got, I took the bus up to Memphis to see her perform in that show.

[*EMCEE steps out onto the stage.*]

EMCEE: That was Amber, Amber Flame. Give her a big hand, guys. Good job, Amber. And now, for your listening and viewing pleasure, direct from Hollywood, California, our very own beatnik beauty, let's give a big round of applause to the luscious [7] Bobbie Dylan. [8]

	[*The curtain opens, revealing Jenny as she sits on a stool on the stage. She holds a guitar up and begins to play. She is topless.*]
JENNY:	(sings) *"Yes, and how many seas must the white dove sail, before she sleeps in the sand."*
FORREST(V.O.):	Her dream had come true. She was a folk singer.[9]
JENNY:	(sings) *"Yes, how many times must the cannonballs fly before they're forever banned." "The answer, my friend is blowing in the wind. The answer is blowing in…"*
	[*Jenny kicks his hand. He yells angrily as he sits back down, then tosses his drink on her.*]
JENNY:	Hey! Hey! Stupid jerk! [10] I'm singing a song here. Polly, get out here! Shut up! Oh, shut up!
	[*Forrest walks up to Man #5 and grabs him and tosses him down on the ground. Man #4 tries to grab Forrest, but Forrest shoves him down too.*]
	Forrest, what are you doing here?
	What are you doing?

---

7) 관능적인
8) 1960년대 미국의 포크 가수, 그의 이름을 모방하여 지은 싸구려 가수.
9) 포크 싱어가 되려던 그녀의 꿈이 드디어 이루어졌다.
10) 바보 같은 놈!: (idiot, moron, or imbecile, and in certain contexts, asshole or bastard.)

TOPICs to DISCUSS

Read the following review and develop your own idea.

> Discuss symbolic implication of the popular song, "Blowing in the Wind."
>
> Much of the film is about the country's pain over having its innocence ripped away in that era by war and civil strife and how, in Forrest Gump, the child lived on. He's our glimpse of a way to have weathered the winds of change, to have risen on their fierce currents and landed in one piece with our souls intact.
>
> *– Robert Faires*

Jenny in Trouble

SITUATIONs 4.

Warming-up Questions & Listening Practice

1. *What does Jenny want Forrest to do?*

   "Forrest, you stay away from me, okay? You just stay away from me, please."
   "What are you doing? Forrest, let me down! You can't keep doing this, Forrest."

2. *Why did Forrest try to rescue Jenny?*

   "You can't keep tryin' to rescue me all the time."
   "They was tryin' to grab you. I can't help it. I love you."

3. *What did Jenny say to Forrest about their love?*

   "Forrest, you don't know what love is.
   You remember that time we prayed, Forrest?
   We prayed for God to turn me into a bird so I could fly far, far away?"

Episode 3. The Answer Is Blowing In the Wind

4. *What did Forrest say when she was about to leave him?*

   "Nothing. I gotta get outta here."
   "So bye-bye, Jenny. They sendin' me to Vietnam. It's this whole other country."

5. *What did Jenny ask Forrest to promise when he was going to Vietnam war?*

   "Just hang on a minute. Listen, you promise me something, okay? Just if you're ever in trouble, don't try to be brave, you just run, okay? Just run away."

🎧 Listen to the audio and check!

FORREST:	Come on.
JENNY:	What are you doing? Forrest, let me down! You can't keep doing this, Forrest. You can't keep tryin' to rescue me all the time.
FORREST:	They was tryin' to grab [11] you.
JENNY:	A lot of people try to grab me. Just–you can't keep doing this all the time!
FORREST:	I can't help it. I love you.
JENNY:	Forrest, you don't know what love is. You remember that time we prayed, Forrest? We prayed for God to turn me into a bird so I could fly far, far away?
FORREST:	Yes, I do.
JENNY:	You think I can fly off this bridge?
FORREST:	What do you mean, Jenny?
JENNY:	Nothing. I gotta get outta here.
FORREST:	But wait. Jenny!
JENNY:	Forrest, you stay away from me, okay? You just stay away

11) to hold, restrain or perhaps seize suddenly.

	from me, please. [*A pickup truck pulls over as Jenny looks at the driver.*]
JENNY:	Can I have a ride?
DRIVER:	Where you going?
JENNY:	I don't care.
DRIVER:	Get in the truck.
FORREST:	So bye-bye, Jenny. They sendin' me to Vietnam. It's this whole other country. [*Jenny walks toward Forrest. She looks at the driver.*]
JENNY:	Just hang on a minute. Listen, you promise me something, okay? Just if you're ever in trouble, don't try to be brave, you just run, okay? Just run away.
FORREST:	Okay. Jenny, I'll write you all the time.
	[*Jenny takes a last look at Forrest, then climbs into the truck. Forrest watches Jenny in the pickup as it drives away.*]
FORREST(V.O.):	And just like that, she was gone.

TOPICs to DISCUSS

Read the following review and develop your own idea.

> Forrest's journey through American history is juxtaposed against the journey taken by his childhood sweetheart, Jenny, a beautiful and intelligent girl whose victimization at the hands of an alcoholic father sends her down a road populated by a series of abusive lovers, drugs, and discontent. Jenny and Forrest's paths constantly cross throughout the years, yet their journeys are separate and distinct. Through the counterculture in the 1960s and eventually the cocaine-fueled disco scene of the 1970s, Jenny is the lost soul who never finds her footing until she is with Forrest, who turns out to be the rock.

Episode 4

We all Have a Destiny

He Was My Lieutenant

SITUATIONs 1

Warming-up Questions & Listening Practice

1. *How was Vietnam like?*

   Now, they told us that Vietnam was gonna be very different from the United Sates of America. Except for all the beer cans and the barbecue, it was.

2. *What is Bubba's plan in Vietnam after they win the war?*

   They tell me these Vietnams is good shrimp. You know, after we win this war, and we take over everything. We can get American shrimpers to come on here and shrimp these waters.

3. *When Lt Dan met Forrest and Bubba, why didn't he want them to salute him?*

   Ho! Get your hands down. Do not salute me.

There are goddamned snipers all around this area who would love to grease an officer.

4. *Why did Dan want Bubba to tuck in big lips?*

   Yeah, well, you better tuck that in. Gonna get that caught on a trip wire.

5. *What did Dan want Forrest and Bubba to do in order to be safe?*

   Look, it's pretty basic here. You stick with me, you learn from the guys who been in country awhile, you'll be right.

6. *Why did Forrest feel lucky Dan was his lieutenant?*

   Lt. Dan sure knew his stuff. I felt real lucky he was my lieutenant. He was from a long, great military tradition. Somebody in his family had fought and died in every single American war.

Listen to the audio and check!

VIETNAM/ MEKONG DELTA

FORREST(V.O.): Now, they told us that Vietnam was gonna be very different from the United Sates of America. Except for all the beer cans and the barbecue, it was.

BUBBA: Y'know, I bet there's shrimp all in these waters. They tell me these Vietnams is good shrimp. You know, after we win this war, and we take over everything. We can get American shrimpers to come on here and shrimp these waters. We'll just shrimp all the time, man. So much shrimp, why, you wouldn't believe it.

LT. DAN: You must be my F.N.G.'s.[1]

BUBBA AND FORREST: Morning', sir!

LT. DAN: Ho! Get your hands down. Do not salute me. There are goddamned snipers all around this area who would love to grease[2] an officer. I'm Lieutenant Dan Taylor. Welcome to

---

1) Fun and Games의 약자. 사이버 오락게임의 동호인 모임을 빗대어 소대장이 포리스트와 버바를 자신의 소속 부대원임을 지칭하는 말.
2) kill(죽이다)의 속어

	Fourth Platoon. [*to Bubba*] What's wrong with your lips?
BUBBA:	I was born with big gums, sir.
LT. DAN:	Yeah, well, you better tuck that in. Gonna get that caught on a trip wire.³⁾ Where you boys from in the world?
BUBBA & FORREST:	Alabama, sir!
LT. DAN:	You twins?
FORREST:	No, we are not relations, sir.
LT. DAN:	Look, it's pretty basic here. You stick with me, you learn from the guys who been in country awhile, you'll be right. There is one item of G.I. gear⁴⁾ that can be the difference between a live grunt⁵⁾ and a dead grunt. Socks, cushion sole, O.D. green. Try and keep your feet dry when we're out humpin'. I want you boys to remember to change your socks wherever we stop. The Mekong will eat a grunt's feet right off his legs.
FORREST(V.O.):	Lt. Dan sure knew his stuff. I felt real lucky he was my lieutenant. He was from a long, great military tradition. Somebody in his family had fought and died in every single American war.

---

3) 덫의 철사
4) 미군이 갖춰야 할 장비(생존을 위해)
5) (미군 속어) 보병, 해병

TOPICs to DISCUSS

Read the following review and develop your own idea.

> The relationship between Forrest and Lt. Dan is one of the movie's most fascinating; it is much like Forrest's relationship with Jenny, in that Forrest is the unwavering rock to which he can always anchor. Yet, Lt. Dan is ultimately the more interesting character because his problems are not so easily reducible to the aftermath of childhood abuse. Rather, he is a genuinely angry character whose bitterness is mostly of his own making because he put too much stock in what he believed to be his "destiny." That he finally comes to peace with himself in the end is further testament to the movie's optimistic outlook, that all will eventually be right in the world despite its seeming randomness.

Forrest's Ping-pong

SITUATIONs 2

Warming-up Questions & Listening Practice

1. *What is the secret to ping-pong that the soldier gave to Forrest?*

   Now the secret to this game is, no matter what happens, never, never take your eye off the ball.

2. *How much did Forrest practice playing ping-pong?*

   So I started playing it all the time. I played ping-pong even when I didn't have anyone to play ping-pong with.

3. *What did the hospital's people say about Forrest's playing ping-pong?*

   The hospital's people said it made me look like a duck in water, whatever that means.

4. *What is Lieutenant Dan's attitude toward a destiny?*

Episode 4. We all Have a Destiny

Now, you listen to me. We all have a destiny. Nothing just happens, it's all part of a plan.

5. *Why does Dan think that he should have died out there with his men?*

   I should have died out there with my men! But now, I'm nothing but a goddamned cripple!

6. *What does Dan want Forrest to imagine?*

   Look! Look! Look at me! Do you see that? Do you know what it's like not to be able to use your legs?

7. *Why does Dan think Forrest cheated him?*

   You cheated me. I had a destiny. I was supposed to die in the field! With honor! That was my destiny! And you cheated me out of it! You understand what I'm saying, Gump? This wasn't supposed to happen. Not to me.

Listen to the audio and check!

SOLDIER: Good catch, Gump. You know how to play this? [*Forrest shakes his head.*]
Come on, let me show you. Here. Now the secret to this game is, no matter what happens, never, never take your eye off the ball. All right…

FORREST(V.O.): For some reason, ping pong came very natural to me.

SOLDIER: See, any idiot can play.

FORREST(V.O.): So I started playing it all the time. I played ping-pong even when I didn't have anyone to play ping-pong with.
The hospital's people said it made me look like a duck in [6] water, whatever that means. Even Lieutenant Dan would come and watch me play.
I played ping-pong so much, I even played it in my sleep. *Lt. Dan stares out the window. Forrest lies in his bed asleep. A hand reaches and grabs him. Lt. Dan pulls Forrest to the floor, and holds Forrest down.*

LT. DAN: Now, you listen to me. We all have a destiny. Nothing just happens, it's all part of a plan. I should have died out there

---

6) Ping Pong made me look like a duck in water: 물 만난 고기처럼 자연스럽게 탁구를 잘 했다.

Episode 4. We all Have a Destiny

	with my men! But now, I'm nothing but a goddamned cripple! A legless freak.[7] Look! Look! Look at me! Do you see that? Do you know what it's like not to be able to use your legs?
FORREST:	Well… Yes, sir, I do.
LT. DAN:	Did you hear what I said? You cheated me. I had a destiny.[8] I was supposed to die in the field! With honor! That was my destiny! And you cheated me out of it!
	You understand what I'm saying, Gump? This wasn't supposed to happen. Not to me. I had a destiny. I was Lieutenant Dan Tayler.
FORREST:	Yo-You're still Lieutenant Dan.
LT. DAN:	Look at me. What am I gonna do now? What am I gonna do now?

---

7) 다리 없어 흉한 병신
8) 내 나름의 운명이 있었다.

TOPICs to DISCUSS

Think about man's destiny by referring to what the two men say like the following.

... **A** "For some reason, ping pong came very natural to me. So I started playing it all the time. I played ping-pong even when I didn't have anyone to play ping-pong with."

... **B** "I was supposed to die in the field! With honor! That was my destiny! And you cheated me out of it!"

Jenny Wanted to Expand her Mind

SITUATIONs 3.

Warming-up Questions & Listening Practice

1. *What does Jenny think of Forrest's uniform?*

   That uniform is a trip, Forrest. You look handsome in it. You do.

2. *What did Forrest and Jenny talk about while they were walking around all night.*

   We walked around all night, Jenny and me, just talkin'.
   She told me about all the travellin' she's done.

3. *What did Jenny try to discover? And what did she try to learn? For that purpose, where did she go?*

   She told me about all the travellin' she's done, and how she'd discovered ways to expand her mind and learn how to live in harmony, which must be out west somewhere, 'cause she made it all the way to California.

Forrest Gump 영화읽기

4. *What is Forrest's opinion about Jennny going West? And what is Jenny's response?*

   You know what I think? I think you should go home to Greenbow. Alabama!

5. *Why didn't Jenny accept Forrest's suggestion that she should go to Alabama?*

   Forrest, we have very different lives, you know.

6. *What gift did Forrest give to Jenny, and why?*

   I got it just by doing what you told me to do.

Listen to the audio and check!

WASHINGTON MONUMENT/ PROTESTER'S ENCAMPMENT–NIGHT.
[They walk in silence. Jenny touches Forrest's uniform.]

JENNY: That uniform is a trip, Forrest.[9] You look handsome in it. You do.
FORREST: You know what?
JENNY: What?
FORREST: I'm glad we were here together in our nation's capitol.
JENNY: Me too, Forrest.
FORREST(V.O.): We walked around all night, Jenny and me, just talkin'. She told me about all the travellin' she's done, and how she'd discovered ways to expand her mind and learn how to live in harmony, which must be out west somewhere, 'cause she made it all the way to California. *[A young hippie looks over his faded Volkswagen at the girls.]*
YOUNG HIPPIE: *Hey, if anybody want to go to San Francisco?*
JENNY: *I'll go.*
YOUNG HIPPIE: *Far out!*

9) 네 유니폼 참 특이하고 멋있다.

FORREST(V.O.):	It was a very special night for the two of us. I didn't want it to end. [*Jenny prepares to board a bus back to Berkeley.*]
FORREST:	I wish you wouldn't go, Jenny.
JENNY:	I have to, Forrest.
FORREST:	You know what I think? I think you should go home to Greenbow. Alabama!
JENNY:	Forrest, we have very different lives, you know. [*Forrest pulls his Medal of Honor from around his neck.*]
FORREST:	I want you to have this.
JENNY:	Forrest, I can't keep this.
FORREST:	I got it just by doing what you told me to do.
JENNY:	Why're you so good to me?

FORREST:	You're my girl.
JENNY:	I'll always be your girl.
FORREST(V.O.):	And just like that, she was gone out of my life again.

Episode 4. We all Have a Destiny

TOPICs to DISCUSS

Talk about Jenny's way of life and the historical background of 1960s in the United States.

I Was a National Celebrity

SITUATIONs 4.

WATCH the MOVIE

Warming-up Questions & Listening Practice

1. *Why did Forrest play ping-pong instead of going back to Vietnam to fight communists?*

   I thought I was going back to Vietnam, but instead, they decided the best way for me to fight communists was to play ping-pong.

2. *What did Forrest do in the Special Services for the wounded veterans?*

   So I was in the Special Services, traveling around the country cheering up all them wounded veterans and showing them how to play ping-pong.

3. *What did Forrest get as a result of the best ping-pong player?*

   I was so good that some years later, the Army decided I should be on the All-American Ping-Pong Team.

Episode 4. We all Have a Destiny

4. *Why did people think that world peace was in the hands of ping-pong players?*

We were the first Americans to visit the land of China in like a million years or something like that, and somebody said that world peace was in our hands.

5. *What had Forrest become when he got home after playing ping-pong?*

But all I did was play ping-pong. When I got home, I was national celebrity, famouser even than Captain Kangaroo.

6. *What did Forrest answer to the question, "Can you, uh, tell us, uh, what was China like?"*

Well, in the land of China, people hardly got nothing at all. And in China, they never go to church.

7. *How did John Lennon, a famous singer die? Why?*

Some years later, that nice young man from England was on his way home to see his little boy and was signing some autographs.
For no particular reason at all, somebody shot him.

Listen to the audio and check!

[*Forrest demonstrates a ping-pong to some wounded vets.*]

FORREST(V.O.): I thought I was going back to Vietnam, but instead, they decided the best way for me to fight communists was to play ping-pong. So I was in the Special Services, traveling around the country cheering up all them wounded veterans and showing them how to play ping-pong. I was so good that some years later, the Army decided I should be on the All-American Ping-Pong Team. We were the first Americans to visit the land of China in like a million years or something like that, and somebody said that world peace was in our hands. But all I did was play ping-pong. When I got home, I was national celebrity, famouser even than Captain Kangaroo.[10]

[*Color footage of the DICK CAVETT Show. Dick Cavett stands up as he introduces Forrest.*]

DICK CAVETT: Here he is, Forrest Gump, right here. Mr. Gump, have a seat.

10) 집에 와보니 텔레비전에 나오는 캥거루 선생보다 전국적으로 더 유명한 명사가 되어 있었다.

	Forrest Gump, John Lennon.
JOHN LENNON:	Welcome home.
DICK CAVETT:	You had quite a trip. Can you, uh, tell us, uh, what was China like?
FORREST:	Well, in the land of China, people hardly got nothing at all.
JOHN LENNON:	No possessions?
FORREST:	And in China, they never go to church.
JOHN LENNON:	No religion, too?
DICK CAVETT:	Oh. Hard to imagine.
JOHN LENNON:	Well, it's easy if you try, Dick.
FORREST(V.O.):	Some years later, that nice young man from England was on his way home to see his little boy and was signing some autographs. For no particular reason at all, somebody shot him.

TOPICs to DISCUSS

Read the following review and develop your own idea.

> Forrest Gump, through no effort of his own, continually finds himself in the middle of important, influential events—initiating the Watergate scandal, for instance, or inspiring John Lennon to write "Imagine." Some criticize Gump as being anti-intellectual for giving a simpleton such central roles in so many crucial moments in time. But we can find Forrest's involvement as a metaphor for how we all move through time. Forrest may be causing and witnessing history without understanding what he does and sees, but so do we all—we can never know the full ramifications of all we do at the moment we do it, and events later recognized as pivotal don't always seem that way at the time, even to those of us far more intelligent and self-aware than Forrest.

Episode 5

A Promise Is a Promise

I always Try to Keep Promise

SITUATIONs 1.

Warming-up Questions & Listening Practice

1. *What didn't Forrest expect to find?*

   Now, when I got home, I had no idea that Momma had all sorts of visitors.

2. *What did the visitors want from Forrest?*

   We've had all sorts of visitors, Forrest. Everybody wants you to use their ping-pong stuff.

3. *Why did a man leave a check for $25000?*

   One man even left a check for twenty-five thousand dollars if you'd be agreeable to saying you like using their paddle.
   Oh, Momma. I only like using my own paddle.

4. *Why did Momma want Forrest to hold a paddle?*

   I know that. I know that. But it's twenty-five thousand dollars, Forrest. I thought maybe you could hold it for a while, see if it grows on you.

5. *What was funny about?*

   That Momma, she sure was right. It's funny how things work out.

6. *Why didn't Forrest stay home for long?*

   I didn't stay home for long, because I'd made a promise to Bubba. And I always try to keep my promise.

7. *Why did Forrest go on down to Bayou La Batre?*

   So I went on down to Bayou La Batre to meet Bubba's family and make their introduction.

8. *How did Forrest answer to Bubba's mother's saying, "Are you crazy?"*

   Are you crazy, or just plain stupid?
   Stupid is as stupid does, Mrs. Blue.

1 Listen to the audio and check!

[*GUMP HOUSE*]
FORREST: I'm home, Momma.
MRS. GUMP: I know, I know.
[*Louise, he's here. He's here, everybody!*]
FORREST(V.O.): Now, when I got home, I had no idea that Momma had all sorts of visitors.
MRS. GUMP: We've had all sorts of visitors, Forrest. Everybody wants you to use their ping-pong stuff. One man even left a check for twenty-five thousand dollars if you'd be agreeable to saying you like using their paddle.
FORREST: Oh, Momma.
I only like using my own paddle.
[*to Louise*] Hi, Miss Louise.
LOUISE: Hey, Forrest.
MRS. GUMP: I know that. I know that. But it's twenty-five thousand dollars, Forrest. I thought maybe you could hold it for a while, see if it grows on you.[1]

1) 점점 좋아하게 되다.

FORREST(V.O.):   That Momma, she sure was right. It's funny how things work out.
I didn't stay home for long, because I'd made a promise to Bubba. And I always try to keep my promise. So I went on down to Bayou La Batre to meet Bubba's family and make their introduction.

MRS. BLUE: Are you crazy, or just plain stupid?
FORREST: Stupid is as stupid does, Mrs. Blue.
MRS. BLUE: I guess.

TOPICs to DISCUSS

Read the following review and develop your own idea.

> The movie's seeming connection between low intelligence and innocence would be unsettling if it weren't for Hanks' ability to suggest that Forrest's goodness comes from someplace deep inside his heart that is in no way connected to his ability to understand complex phenomena. The movie makes it clear that Forrest never fully comprehends everything that happens around him, yet that has little bearing on how he treats the people he loves.

Shrimping Business

SITUATIONs 2.

Warming-up Questions & Listening Practice

1. *What did Forrest do at Bubba's grave?*

   And of course, I paid my respect to Bubba himself.

2. *What did Forrest say at Bubba's grave?*

   Hey, Bubba, it's me, Forrest Gump. I remember everything you said, and I got it all figured out.

3. *How much money did Forrest bring to Bubba's grave?*

   I'm taking the twenty-four thousand, five hundred and six-two dollars and forty-seven cents that I got.

4. *For what did Forrest spend that money?*

   Well, that's left after a new hair cut and a new suit and I took Momma

Episode 5. A Promise Is a Promise

out to real fancy dinner and I bought a bus ticket and three Doctor Peppers.

5. *How did Forrest make that money?*

   Well, that's what's left after me saying, "When I was in China on the All-America Ping-Pong Team, I just loved playing ping-pong with my Flex-O-Ping-Pong Paddle."

6. *What is it that Momma says is a little white lie?*

   Everybody knows it isn't true, but Momma says it's just a little white lie so it wouldn't hurt nobody.

7. *How did Forrest use that money?*

   So, anyway, I'm putting all that on gas, ropes and new nets and a brand-new shrimpin' boat.

8. *What did Forrest find about shrimping?*

   Now, Bubba had told me everything he knows about shrimpin', but you know what I found out? Shrimpin' is tough.

9. *Why did Forrest come to think about naming the boat?*

   Hey, you ever think about namin' this old boat? It's bad luck to have a boat without a name.

10. *What was the name of the boat that Forrest could think of?*

I'd never named a boat before, but there was only one I could think of. The most beautiful name in the wide world.

🎧 Listen to the audio and check!

[*At BUBBA'S GRAVE*]

FORREST(V.O.): And of course, I paid my respect to Bubba himself. [2]
"Hey, Bubba, it's me, Forrest Gump.
I remember everything you said, and I got it all figured out. I'm taking the twenty-four thousand, five hundred and sixty-two dollars and forty-seven cents that I got. Well, that's left after a new hair cut and a new suit and I took Momma out to real fancy dinner and I bought a bus ticket and three Doctor Peppers." [*Forrest walks along a wooden pier. Forrest pays an old black shrimper a large wad of cash.*]

OLD SHRIMPER: Tell me something. Are you stupid or something?

FORREST: Stupid is as stupid does, sir.

[*At BUBBA'S GRAVE*]

FORREST: Well, that's what's left after me saying, "When I was in China on the All-America Ping-Pong Team, I just loved playing ping-pong with my Flex-O-Ping-Pong Paddle." Everybody knows it isn't true,[3] but Momma says it's just a

2) Bubba의 묘소에서 참배했다.
3) 포리스트가 25000불 광고료를 받고 사용하기로 동의한 탁구 패들 상표.

little white lie so it wouldn't hurt nobody.⁴⁾ So, anyway, I'm putting all that on gas, ropes and new nets and a brand-new shrimpin' boat.

[*Forrest steers his shrimping boat. The boat is old and rusty.*]

FORREST(V.O.): Now, Bubba had told me everything he knows about shrimpin', but you know what I found out? Shrimpin' is tough. I only caught five.

OLD SHRIMPER: A couple of more, you can have yourself a cocktail. Hey, you ever think about namin' this old boat? It's bad luck to have a boat without a name.

FORREST(V.O.): I'd never named a boat before, but there was only one I could think of. The most beautiful name in the wide world.

[*some film clips about Jenny in Sanfrancisco.*]

Now, I hadn't heard from Jenny in a long while. But I thought about her a lot. And I hoped that whatever she was doing made her happy. I thought about Jenny all the time.

[*At BAYOU DOCK*]

---

4) Everyone knew it wasn't true: It was just a little white lie: 누구라도 사실이 아니라는 것을 알고 있었지만 근본적으로 남을 해치지 않은 거짓말.

Episode 5. A Promise Is a Promise

TOPICs to DISCUSS

Discuss what the following sayings indicate by referring to the events of the above film clip.

"Tell me something. Are you stupid or something?"
"Stupid is as stupid does, sir."

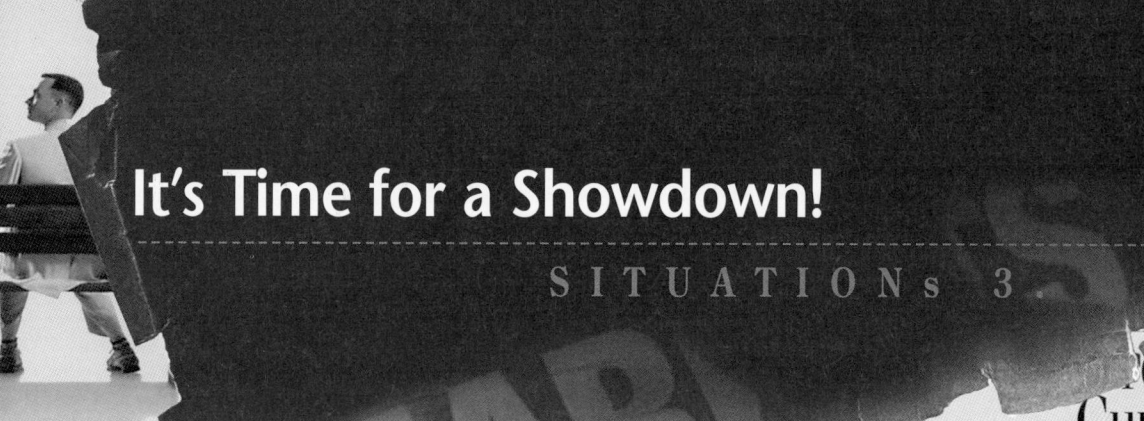

It's Time for a Showdown!

SITUATIONs 3

Warming-up Questions & Listening Practice

1. *What did Lieutenant Dan do at the Bayou dock?*

    Lieutenant Dan, what are you doing here?
    Well, I thought I'd try out my sea legs.

2. *Why did Lieutenant Dan come to the Bayou dock?*

    Yes, I know that. You wrote me a letter, you idiot. Well, well, Captain Forrest Gump. I had to see this for myself.

3. *What does Lieutenant mean by saying "a man of my word"?*

    And I told you if you were ever a shrimp boat captain, that I'd be your first mate. Well, here I am. I am a man of my word.

Episode 5. A Promise Is a Promise

4. *What did Lieutenant Dan ask Forrest not to expect?*

   Yeah, but don't you be thinking that I'm gonna be calling you sir.

5. *Where did Lieutenant Dan lead the ship to find some shrimp?*

   I have a feeling if we head due east, we'll find some shrimp! So, take a left! Take a left!

6. *What did Forrest do when he could not catch shrimps?*

   So I went to church every Sunday. Sometimes Lieutenant Dan came, too, though I think he left the praying up to me.

7. *Why was Lieutenant Dan's saying about God funny?*

   It's funny Lieutenant Dan said that, 'cause right then, God showed up.

8. *How did Dan and Forrest react to the storm?*

   Now me, I was scared. But Lieutenant Dan, he was mad.

9. *How did Lieutenant Dan confront?*

   Come on! You call this a storm? Blow, you son-of-a-bitch! Blow! It's time for a showdown! You and me. I'm right here. Come and get me! You'll never sink this boat!

🎧 Listen to the audio and check!

FORREST:	Hi! Lieutenant Dan, what are you doing here?
LT. DAN:	Well, I thought I'd try out my sea legs.
FORREST:	Well, you ain't got no legs, Lieutenant Dan.
LT. DAN:	Yes, I know that. You wrote me a letter, you idiot. Well, well, Captain Forrest Gump. I had to see this for myself. And I told you if you were ever a shrimp boat captain, that I'd be your first mate. Well, here I am. I am a man of my word.[5]
FORREST:	Okay.
LT. DAN:	Yeah, but don't you be thinking that I'm gonna be calling you sir.
FORREST:	No, sir. [*pointing to his boat*] That's my boat!
LT. DAN:	I have a feeling if we head due east, we'll find some shrimp! So, take a left! Take a left!
FORREST:	Which way?
LT. DAN:	Over there! They're over there! Get, get on the wheel and take a left!

5) I'll be your first mate. I am a man of my word: 내가 자네의 1등 항해사가 되어 주겠다. 나는 약속을 지키는 사람이지.

Episode 5. A Promise Is a Promise

FORREST:	Okay.
LT. DAN:	Gump, what are you doing? Take a left! Left! That's where we're gonna find those shrimp, my boy! That's where we'll find 'em.
FORREST:	Still no shrimp, Lieutenant Dan.
LT. DAN:	Okay, so I was wrong.
FORREST:	Well, how we gonna find them?
LT. DAN:	Well, maybe you should just pray for shrimp.
FORREST(V.O.):	So I went to church every Sunday. Sometimes Lieutenant Dan came, too, though I think he left the praying up to me.
FORREST:	No shrimp.
LT. DAN:	Where the hell's this God of yours?
FORREST(V.O.):	It's funny Lieutenant Dan said that, 'cause right then, God showed up.
LT. DAN:	You'll never sink this boat!
FORREST(V.O.):	Now me, I was scared. But Lieutenant Dan, he was mad.
LT. DAN:	Come on! You call this a storm? Blow, you son-of-a-bitch! Blow! It's time for a showdown! You and me. I'm right here. Come and get me! You'll never sink this boat! [*An ANCHORMAN over TV, is standing in front of a pier.*]

TOPICs to DISCUSS

Read the following review and develop your own idea.

> Gump, mildly retarded, is naive, but knows the difference between right and wrong. He also knows what love is. He walks the straight and narrow, while everyone around him goes spinning off in various directions on those turbulent times.
>
> The theme of the film is an exploration of the well-known philosophical dichotomy between free-will and predestination. Gump decides life contains elements of both, but the story is so far-fetched it's hard to make a case for either viewpoint.
>
> – by Robert Roten

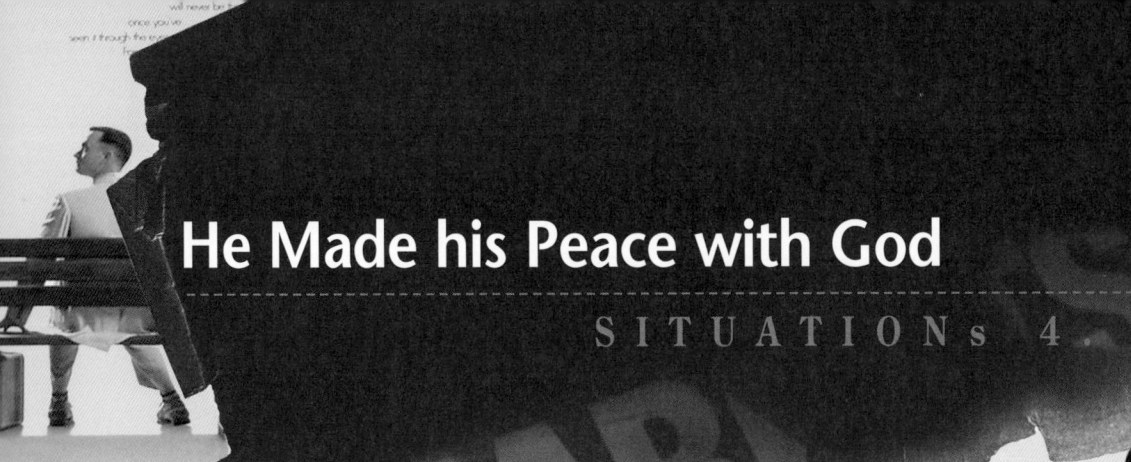

He Made his Peace with God

SITUATIONs 4

Warming-up Questions & Listening Practice

1. *What happened yesterday? How did it destroy everything?*

   Hurricane Carmen came through here yesterday destroying nearly everything in its path.

2. *How did the storm influence on the shrimping industry?*

   And as in other towns up and down the coast,
   Bayou La Batre's entire shrimping industry has fallen victim to Carmen and has been left in utter ruin.

3. *What was the special news about one shrimping boat?*

   Speaking with local officials, this reporter has learned, in fact, only one shrimping boat actually survived the storm.

4. *How was Forrest's shrimping after the storm?*
    Why was his business easy?

    After that, shrimpin' was easy. And since people still needed them shrimps for shrimp cocktails and barbecues and all and we were the only boat left standing "Bubba-Gump" shrimp's what they got.

5. *Was Forrest's shrimping business a success? If so, how?*

    We got a whole bunch of boats, twelve Jenny's, a big ol' warehouse. We even have hats that says "Bubba-Gump" on 'em. "Bubba-Gump Shrimp." It's a household name.

6. *What did an old gentleman say after he heard Forrest's story?*

    Hold on there, boy. Are you telling me you're the owner of the Bubba-Gump Shrimp Corporation?

7. *Did the old gentleman believe in Forrest's story?*
    If not, what did he say?

    Boy, I've heard some whoppers in my time, but that tops them all. We was sitting next to a millionaire!

8. *What did the old woman say after she heard Forrest's story?*
    Do you think she believed in his story?

    Well, I thought it was a very lovely story. And you tell it so well, with such enthusiasm.

Episode 5. A Promise Is a Promise

9. What did Dan thank Forrest for?
And how did Forrest interpret Dan's attitude?

Forrest, I never thanked you for saving my life.
He never actually said so, but I think he made his peace with God.

Listen to the audio and check!

	[*over television*]
ANCHORMAN:	Hurricane Carmen came through here yesterday destroying nearly everything in its path. And as in other towns up and down the coast, Bayou La Batre's entire shrimping industry has fallen victim to Carmen [6] and has been left in utter ruin. Speaking with local officials, this reporter has learned, in fact, only one shrimping boat actually survived the storm. [*Forrest's mother shouts to find her son on T.V, "Louise, that's Forrest!"*]
FORREST(V.O.):	After that, shrimpin' was easy. And since people still needed them shrimps for shrimp cocktails and barbecues and all and we were the only boat left standing "Bubba-Gump" shrimp's what they got. We got a whole bunch of boats, twelve Jenny's, a big ol' warehouse. We even have hats that says "Bubba-Gump" on 'em. "Bubba-Gump Shrimp." It's a household name.[7] [*The man sitting on the bench listens to Forrest. An*

---

6) The entire shipping industry has fallen victim to Hurricane Carmen: 새우 잡이 사업이 태풍 카멘의 희생물이 되었다. 태풍으로 인해 파괴되었다는 뜻.
7) 가정집에 널리 알려진 유명 제품.

Episode 5. A Promise Is a Promise

	ELDERLY WOMAN *sits next to the man.*]
MAN:	Hold on there, boy. Are you telling me you're the owner of the Bubba-Gump Shrimp Corporation?
FORREST:	Yes, sir. We've got more money than Davy Crocket.
MAN:	Boy, I've heard some whoppers in my time, but that tops them all.[8] We was sitting next to a millionaire!
ELDERLY WOMAN:	Well, I thought it was a very lovely story. And you tell it so well, with such enthusiasm.
FORREST:	Would you like to see what Lieutenant Dan looks like?
ELDERLY WOMAN:	Well, yes, I would! [*Forrest shows her the cover of a "Fortune" magazine*]
FORREST:	That's him right there. And let me tell you something about Lieutenant Dan. [*At BOAT/DECK*]
LT. DAN:	Forrest, I never thanked you for saving my life.
FORREST(V.O.):	He never actually said so, but I think he made his peace with God.

TOPICs to DISCUSS

- Discuss how Forrest overcame his handicap and the natural disaster.
- Discuss how Lieutenant Dan overcame his handicap and his destiny.

---

8) I've heard some stories, but that tops them all: 지금까지 들은 이야기 중에서 가장 믿기 어려운 이야기이다.

Episode 6

Do the Best with What God Gave You

Mother Dying

SITUATIONs 1.

Warming-up Questions & Listening Practice

1. *Explain about Mother's attitude toward death.*

   It's my time. It's just my time. Oh, now, don't you be afraid, sweetheart. Death is just a part of life. It's something we're all destined to do.

2. *What did Mother think of her destiny?*

   I didn't know it, but I was destined to be your momma. I did the best I could.

3. *What is Mother's advice about Forrest's destiny?*

   Well, I happened to believe you make your own destiny. You have to do the best with what God gave you.
   You're gonna have to figure that out for yourself.

4. *How did Forrest's mother describe life?*

   Life is a box of chocolates, Forrest.
   You never know what you're gonna get.

5. *What gift did Forrest buy for his mother?*

   She had got the cancer and died on a Tuesday.
   I bought her a new hat with little flowers on it.

Listen to the audio and check!

Forrest runs past the row of mailboxes and turns into the drive.

FORREST: Where's Momma?

LOUISE: She's upstairs. [*Forrest opens the door, the doctor stands next to Mrs. Gump in bed.*]

MRS. GUMP: Hi, Forrest.

DOCTOR: I'll see you tomorrow.

MRS. GUMP: Oh, all right.

[*The doctor looks down at Forrest's legs.*]

DOCTOR: We sure got you straightened out, didn't we, boy? [1]

[*The doctor leaves and closes the door.*]

FORREST: What's the matter, Momma?

MRS. GUMP: I'm dyin', Forrest. Come on in, sit down over here.

FORREST: Why are you dyin', Momma?

MRS. GUMP: It's my time. It's just my time. Oh, now, don't you be afraid, sweetheart. Death is just a part of life. It's something we're all destined to do.[2] I didn't know it, but I was destined to be your momma. I did the best I could.

1) 포리스트 검프가 어린 시절 구부러진 등을 펴는 치료를 했다는 뜻.
2) 죽음이란 단지 삶의 일부이다. 어차피 우리 모두가 맞아야 할 과정이다.

FORREST:	You did good, Momma.
MRS. GUMP:	Well, I happened to believe you make your own destiny. You have to do the best with what God gave you.
FORREST:	What's my destiny, Momma?
MRS. GUMP:	You're gonna have to figure that out for yourself. 3) **Life is a box of chocolates, Forrest. You never know what you're gonna get.**
FORREST(V.O.):	Momma always had a way of explaining things so I could understand them.
MRS. GUMP:	I will miss you, Forrest.
FORREST(V.O.):	She had got the cancer and died on a Tuesday. I bought her a new hat with little flowers on it.

3) 네 스스로 운명을 만들어 나가야 할 것이다.

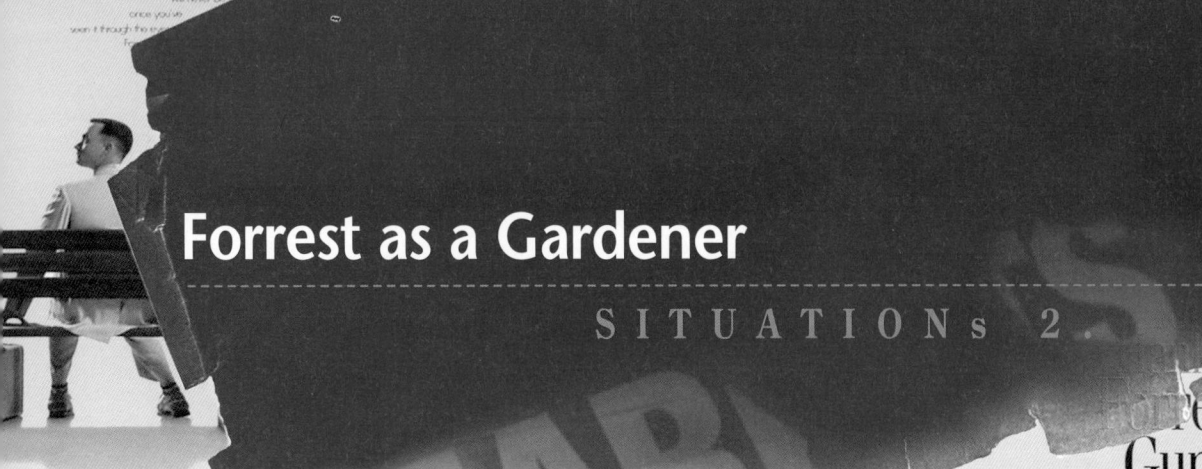

Forrest as a Gardener

SITUATIONs 2

Warming-up Questions & Listening Practice

1. *Why did not the elderly woman take the Number Seven bus?*

   There'll be another one along shortly.

2. *Choose the ones which are not related with Forrest.*

   I had been a football star, and a war hero, and a national celebrity, and a shrimpin' boat captain, and a college graduate, a lawn tractor

3. *Who take care of Forrest's money? And how?*

   I never went back to work for Lieutenant Dan, though he did take care of my Bubba-Gump money. He got me invested in some kind of fruit company.

Forrest Gump 영화읽기

4. *What is Mother's advice about fortune?*

   Now, Momma said there's only so much fortune a man really needs and the rest is just for showing off.

5. *What did Forrest do with the rest of the money?*

   So, I gave a whole bunch of it to the Four Square Gospel Church. And I gave a whole bunch to the Bayou La Batre Fishing Hospital.

6. *Why didn't Bubba's mother have to work in anybody's kitchen any more?*

   And even though Bubba was dead, and Lieutenant Dan said I was nuts. I gave Bubba's mommy Bubba's share.

Listen to the audio and check!

The elderly woman and Forrest sit. The woman is crying and wipes her eyes with a hankie.

FORREST: And that's all I have to say about that.

[*A bus stops.*]

FORREST: Didn't you say you were waiting for the Number Seven bus?

WOMAN: There'll be another one along shortly.

FORREST: Now, because I had been a football star, and a war hero, and a national celebrity, and a shrimpin' boat captain, and a college graduate, the city of Greenbow, Alabama, decided to get together and offered me a fine job.

FORREST(V.O.): So, I never went back to work for Lieutenant Dan, though he did take care of my Bubba-Gump money. He got me invested in some kind of fruit company.[4] And so then I got a call from him saying we don't have to worry about money no more.

FORREST: And I said, "That's good. One less thing." Now, Momma

---

4) 1970년대 애플전자 컴퓨터 회사에 투자한 것을 잘못 이해하여 과일회사에 투자한 것이라고 말하고 있다.

said there's only so much fortune a man really needs and the rest is just for showing off. So, I gave a whole bunch of it to the Four Square Gospel Church. And I gave a whole bunch to the Bayou La Batre Fishing Hospital.

And even though Bubba was dead, and Lieutenant Dan said I was nuts. I gave Bubba's mommy Bubba's share.[5]

[*to the elderly woman*] And you know what?[6]

She didn't have to work in nobody's kitchen no more.

TOPICs to DISCUSS

Read the following review and develop your own idea.

> Gump the football hero becomes Gump the Medal of Honor winner in Vietnam, and then Gump the Ping-Pong champion, Gump the shrimp boat captain, Gump the millionaire stockholder (he gets shares in a new "fruit company" named Apple Computer), and Gump the man who runs across America and then retraces his steps.
>
> It could be argued that with his IQ of 75 Forrest does not quite understand everything that happens to him. Not so. He understands everything he needs to know, and the rest, the movie suggests, is just surplus.
>
> *– by Roger Ebert*

[5] 비록 버바는 세상을 떠났고 댄 중위는 저보고 바보라고 했지만, 저는 버바의 몫(회사 투자) 을 그의 어머니에게 드렸습니다.
[6] 무슨 일이 있었는지 말씀드릴까요? 버바의 어머니는 이제 (돈이 많아서) 남의 식당에 가서 일할 필요가 없어졌어요.

Jenny Came Back Home

SITUATIONs 3.

Warming-up Questions & Listening Practice

1. *When would Forrest think of Jenny?*

   But at nighttime, when there was nothing to do and the house was all empty, I'd always think of Jenny.

2. *Why did Forrest think Jenny came back and stayed with him?*

   Jenny came back and stayed with me. Maybe it was because she had nowhere else to go.

3. *What other reason did Forrest think of for which Jenny came back to him?*

   Or maybe it was because she was so tired, because she went to bed and slept and slept like she hadn't slept in years.

4. *What does Forrest think of having Jenny home?*

   It was wonderful having her home.

5. *What did Forrest do every day? How did he talk to Jenny?*

   Every day we'd take a walk, and I'd jabber on like a monkey in a tree.

6. *What did he tell Jenny about? And how did Jenny listen to him?*

   And she'd listen about ping-pong and shrimpin' boats and Momma makin' a trip to heaven. I did all the talkin'. Jenny most of the time was real quiet.

🎧 Listen to the audio and check!

	Forrest looks down the road as he steps onto the porch.
FORREST(V.O.):	But at nighttime, when there was nothing to do and the house was all empty, I'd always think of Jenny.
	Jenny walks across the lawn to Forrest.
FORREST(V.O.):	And then, she was there.
JENNY:	Hello, Forrest.
FORREST:	Hello, Jenny.
FORREST(V.O.):	Jenny came back and stayed with me. Maybe it was because she had nowhere else to go. Or maybe it was because she was so tired, because she went to bed and slept and slept like she hadn't slept in years. It was wonderful having her home. Every day we'd take a walk, and I'd jabber on like a monkey in a tree. And she'd listen about ping-pong and shrimpin' boats and Momma makin' a trip to heaven. I did all the talkin'. Jenny most of the time was real quiet.
FORREST:	…big ol' gobs of rain and little bitty stinging rain and rain…

TOPICs to DISCUSS

Read the following review and develop your own idea.

> Most impressive is Gump's unswerving love for Jenny who first reaches out to him when everyone else in elementary school rejects him. This abused girl turns into a self-destructive woman who samples the worst excesses of the drug counterculture. Gump remains true to her over the years until she blesses him with the best gift of all.
>
> Holy fools are debonair souls whose love, devotion, and delight in life are unalloyed. We are fortunate to have this screen version of one of their number. Hopefully, Forrest Gump will encourage many of us to express aspects of the holy fool inside ourselves.
>
> – by Frederic and Mary Ann Brussat

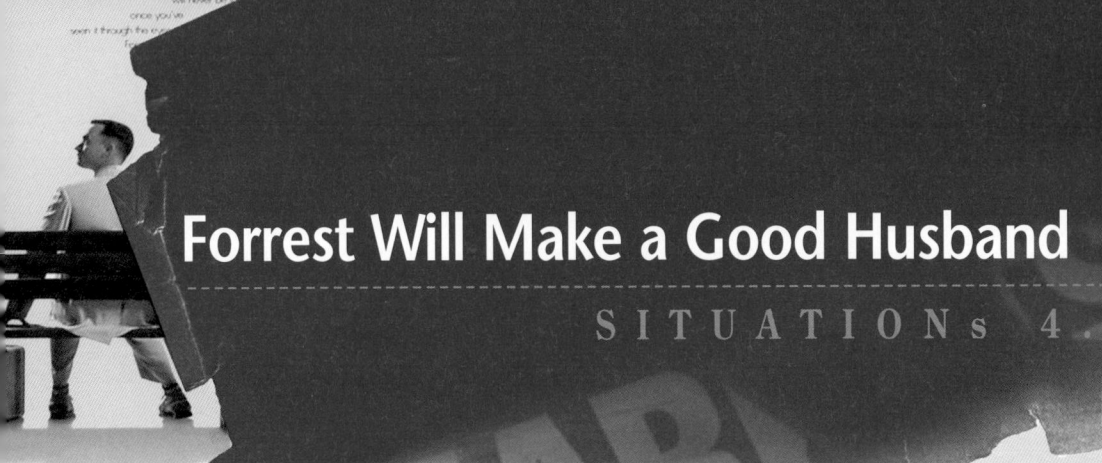

Forrest Will Make a Good Husband

SITUATIONs 4.

WATCH the MOVIE

Warming-up Questions & Listening Practice

1. *What do you think is the reason for which Jenny throws stones at her saying "how could you do this?"*

   How could you do this?
   Sometimes I guess there just aren't enough rocks.

2. *How did Forrest like Jenny's staying with him?*

   I never really knew why she came back, but I didn't care.
   It was like olden times.
   We was like peas and carrots again.

3. *What gift did Forrest and Jenny give to each other?*

   Every day I'd pick pretty flowers and put them in her room for her.
   And she gave me the best gift anyone could ever get in the wide world.

Forrest Gump 영화읽기

4. *What kind of shoes did Jenny give Forrest?*

   They make them just for running.

5. *Why did Forrest and Jenny feel they were like family?*

   And she even showed me how to dance.
   And, well, we was like family, Jenny and me.
   And it was the happiest time of my life.

6. *How did Forrest propose to Jenny?*

   Will you marry me? I'd make a good husband, Jenny.

Listen to the audio and check!

Jenny's old house stands at the end of the dirt road. Jenny suddenly heaves a rock angrily at the house. She throws other things at the house.

JENNY: How could you do this?

[*She breaks a window. Jenny collapses to the ground and sobs.*]

FORREST(V.O.): Sometimes I guess there just aren't enough rocks. I never really knew why she came back, but I didn't care. It was like olden times. We was like peas and carrots again. Every day I'd pick pretty flowers and put them in her room for her. And she gave me the best gift anyone could ever get in the wide world.

JENNY: Okay, you can open your eyes.

FORREST: New shoes!

JENNY: They make them just for running.

FORREST(V.O.): And she even showed me how to dance. And, well, we was like family, Jenny and me. And it was the happiest time of my life.

Forrest and Jenny are watching the 4th of July celebration on TV.

JENNY: You done watching it?

FORREST: Mm-hmm.

JENNY:	I'm going to bed.
FORREST:	Will you marry me? I'd make a good husband, Jenny.
JENNY:	You would, Forrest.
FORREST:	But you won't marry me.
JENNY:	You don't want to marry me.
FORREST:	Why don't you love me, Jenny? I'm not a smart man, but I know what love is.

TOPICs to DISCUSS

Read the following review and develop your own idea.

> *Forrest Gump* certainly plays to the sucker inside all of us, a tale of how a person can overcome any obstacle (even mild retardation!) if he only tries hard enough. Tom Hanks, in an Oscar-winning performance, gives his usual best in the title role, as he rumbles through football games, Vietnam, ping-pong playing, shrimp boat captaining, distance running, and of course, adventures in love with his precious Jenny, who winds up on the wrong side of the tracks. The problem, I think, is that real people have found themselves unable to replicate Forrest's success–and these are people who are not mildly retarded.
>
> – *by Christopher Null*

Episode 7

Put the Past Behind You!

Forrest Began to Run!

SITUATIONs 1.

Warming-up Questions & Listening Practice

1. *Why did Forrest begin to run?*

   That day, for no particular reason, I decided to go for a little run.

2. *What did Forrest think when he ran to the end of the road?*

   So I ran to the end of the road, and when I got there, I thought maybe I'd run to the end of town.

3. *What did Forrest think when he ran to the end of town?*

   And when I got there, I thought maybe I'd just run across Greenbow County.

4. *What did Forrest think when he got to another ocean?*

When I got to another ocean, I figured since I've gone this far, I might as well just turn back, keep right on going.

5. *What did Forrest do when he got tired and hungry while he ran?*

When I got tired, I slept. When I got hungry, I ate.

Listen to the audio and check!

[Forrest sit on a rocking chair with his running shoes on. He runs down the drive away from his house.]

FORREST(V.O.): That day, for no particular reason, I decided to go for a little run. *[Forrest runs to the end of the drive, then turns right and runs down the highway.]* So I ran to the end of the road, and when I got there, I thought maybe I'd run to the end of town. And when I got there, I thought maybe I'd just run across Greenbow County. And I figured since I run this far, maybe I'd just run across the great state of Alabama. And that's what I did I ran clear across Alabama.[1]

[EXT. BUS STOP–PRESENT]

FORREST: For no particular reason, I just kept on going. I ran clear to the ocean.

FORREST(V.O.): And when I got there, I figured since I'd gone this far, I might as well turn around, just keep on going. When I got to another ocean, I figured since I've gone this far, I might

1) 앨라배마 주를 가로질러 곧장 달렸다.

as well just turn back, keep right on going.[2] When I got tired, I slept. When I got hungry, I ate. When I had to go, you know, I went.

TOPICs to DISCUSS
Read the following review and develop your own idea.

> There is a long and fascinating tradition of the holy fool in spiritual literature. These people follow the dictates of the heart and are often able to effect great works of mercy and compassion. Their brand of selflessness is free of reason's madness and the ego's frivolous grandeur. Holy fools pay no heed to the worldly pursuit of power, status, or financial success. That is why they are usually deemed crazy and forced to live as lonely outsiders.

2) (모든 사정을 감안해서) 줄곧 달리는 것이 좋을 것 같다는 생각을 했다.

Forrest Running On TV
SITUATIONs 2

Warming-up Questions & Listening Practice

1. *Whom did Forrest think of while he was running?*

   I'd think a lot about Momma, Bubba, and Lieutenant Dan. Most of all, I thought about Jenny.

2. *How long did Forrest run?*

   For more than two years now, a man named Forrest Gump, a gardener from Greenbow, Alabama, stopping only to sleep, has been running across America.

3. *How many times did Forrest take his journey across America? Where is Forrest going to cross again today?*

   For the fourth time on his journey across America, Forrest Gump, a gardener from Greenbow, Alabama, is about to cross the Mississippi

River again today.

4. *What did Jenny say when she watched Forrest run on TV?*

   I'll be damned. Forrest!

🎧 Listen to the audio and check!

ELDERLY WOMAN:	And so, you just ran?
FORREST:	Yeah. I'd think a lot about Momma and Bubba, and Lieutenant Dan, but most of all, I thought about Jenny. I thought about her a lot. *The three men in the barber shop watch the news on television.*
NEWSCASTER:	For more than two years now, a man named Forrest Gump, a gardener from Greenbow, Alabama, stopping only to sleep, has been running across America.
	INT. COFFEE SHOP *Jenny fills customer's coffee cups.*
NEWSCASTER:	Charles Cooper brings us this report.
NEWSMAN:	For the fourth time on his journey across America, Forrest Gump, a gardener from Greenbow, Alabama, is about to cross the Mississippi River again today.
	[*The TV shows Forrest runs across a bridge that reads "Mississippi River."*]
JENNY:	I'll be damned. Forrest…3)

3) 아이구 맙소사! 어머나!

TOPICs to DISCUSS

Read the following review and develop your own idea.

> Not long after Forrest is depicted watching American bi-centennial celebrations (July 4 1976, presumably) he starts running from sea to shining sea 'for no particular reason'. Furthermore, he stops running just prior to the depiction of the assassination attempt on Reagan, from memory. This means that Forrest was running (remember, 'for no particular reason') for just about exactly the duration of the Carter administration. I guess this explains why Forrest never met President Carter. Is this some sort of comment on the Carter administration (perhaps that America lost its way under Carter- a dubious proposition at best) or simply co-incidence?

Forrest Was Interviewed

SITUATIONs 3

Warming-up Questions & Listening Practice

1. *What are the reasons for which the reporters guess for Forrest's running?*

   Are you doing this for world peace? women's right? for the environment? for animals? for nuclear arms?

2. *Why did the reporters ask Forrest so many questions?*

   They just couldn't believe that somebody would do all that running for no particular reason.

3. *What did Forrest answer for the question, "Why are you running?"*

   I just felt like running.

4. *What does it mean for an alarm to go off in his head?*

   I mean, it was like an alarm went off in my head, you know. said, here's a guy that's got his act together.

5. *How is Forrest described by people?*

   Here's somebody who's got it, all figured out. Here's somebody who has the answer. I'll follow you anywhere, Mr. Gump.

Listen to the audio and check!

[*Newsmen try to interview Forrest while he runs.*]

NEWSMAN 1:	Sir, why are you running?
NEWSMAN 2:	Why are you running?
NEWSMAN 1:	Are you doing this for world peace?
NEWSMAN 3:	Are you doing this for women's right?
NEWSMAN 1:	Or for the environment?
NEWSMAN 2:	Or for animals?
NEWSMAN 3:	Or for nuclear arms?
FORREST(V.O.):	They just couldn't believe that somebody would do all that running for no particular reason.
NEWSMAN 2:	Why are you doing this?
FORREST:	I just felt like running.

EXT. BUS STOP-PRESENT

FORREST:	I just left like running. *Forrest runs as a YOUNG MAN runs up to him.*
YOUNG MAN:	It's you. I can't believe it's really you.

EXT. BUS STOP-PRESENT

FORREST:	Now, for some reason what I was doing seemed to make

Forrest Gump 영화읽기

	sense to people.
YOUNG MAN:	I mean, it was like an alarm went off in my head, you know. I said, "here's a guy that's got his act together. ⁴⁾ Here's somebody who's got it, all figured out. Here's somebody who has the answer." I'll follow you anywhere, Mr. Gump.

TOPICs to DISCUSS
Read the following review and develop your own idea.

> Forrest Gump has several messages, some of which are less obvious than others. The most frequently recurring theme is an admonition not to give up on life. Why surrender when you don't know what lies ahead? By contrasting Forrest's life with the lives of those around him, and by showing how the passage of time brings solace to even the most embittered hearts, the movie underlines this point.
>
> – by James Berardinelli

---

4) It was like an alarm went off in my head: Here's somebody who has got his act together.
마치 경고음이 머리 속에서 울리는 것 같았다. 여기에 바로 자신의 행동을 통해 주변 사람과 공동 사회에 긍정적인 기여를 하는 사람이 있다.

People Joined Forrest in Running
SITUATIONs 4.

Warming-up Questions & Listening Practice

1. *Why did people join in Forrest's running?*

   So, I got company. And after that I got more company. And then, even more people joined in. Somebody later told me it gave people hope.

2. *Who followed Forrest and what did he ask?*

   I was wondering if you might help me, huh?
   Listen, I'm in the bumper sticker business and I've been trying to think up a good slogan.

3. *Why did the man think Forrest could help to think up a good slogan?*

   And since you have been such a big inspiration to the people around here, I thought you might be able to help me…

Forrest Gump 영화읽기

4. *How did the man make money?*

    And some years later I heard that fella did come up with a bumper sticker slogan, he made a lot of money off of it.

5. *How did the man get an idea for his bumper sticker slogan?*

    Whoa! Man, you just ran through a big pile of dogshit!

6. *What is the symbolic implication of "Shit happens"?*

    And some years later I heard that fella did come up with a bumper sticker slogan… A bumper sticker reads "Shit Happens." …and he make a lot of money off of it.

Listen to the audio and check!

FORREST(V.O.): So, I got company. And after that I got more company. And then, even more people joined in. Somebody later told me it gave people hope. Now. Now, I don't know anything about that, but Some of those people asked me if I could help them out.

AGING HIPPIE: Hey, man, hey, listen. I was wondering if you might help me, huh? Listen, I'm in the bumper sticker business and I've been trying to think up a good slogan. And since you have been such a big inspiration to the people around here, I thought you might be able to help me jump into... Whoa! Man, you just ran through a big pile of dogshit!

FORREST: It happens.

AGING HIPPIE: What, shit?

FORREST: Sometimes.

FORREST(V.O.): And some years later I heard that fella did come up with a bumper sticker slogan... *A bumper sticker reads "Shit Happens."* 5) ...and he make a lot of money off of it. *The hippie stops to ponder this profound thought.*

---

5) 인생에는 안 좋은 일도 우연히 일어난다. (Shit happens.); 아마도 이런 표현의 스티커를 자동차 범퍼에 다니는 유행이 시작되어 이 스티커를 만든 사람이 돈을 벌었다는 암시를 하고 있음.

People Want Helps from Forrest

SITUATIONs 5

WATCH the MOVIE

Warming-up Questions & Listening Practice

1. *Who did Forrest meet while he was running?*
   What did the man want Forrest to do?

   Another time I was running along, somebody who had lost all his money in the T-shirt business. and he wanted to put my face on a T-shirt.

2. *How did the man get a help from Forrest?*

   And some years later I found out that man did come up with a idea for a T-shirt and he made a lot of money off of it.

3. *What was the family wisdom that Mother gave to Forrest?*
   What was Forrest's running about?

   My Momma always said you got to put the past behind you before you can move on.

Episode 7. Put the Past Behind You!

4. *How long did Forrest run? And what did he say when his running days was over?*

I had run for three years, two months, fourteen days, and sixteen hours. I'm pretty tired. I think I'll go home now.

🎧 Listen to the audio and check!

FORREST(V.O.): Another time I was running along, somebody who had lost all his money in the T-shirt business, and he wanted to put my face on a T-shirt, but he couldn't draw that well and he didn't have a camera.

WILD-EYED MAN: I think it would be really fortunate for me if I could get your name on these, oh, your face and name on these T-shirts. It would be wonderful. Here, use this one. Nobody likes that color anyway.

Forrest wipes his face on the towel and hands it back to the man.

FORREST: Have a nice day.

The man looks at the T-shirt. He holds it up displaying the "Happy Face."

FORREST(V.O.): And some years later I found out that man did come up with a idea for a T-shirt and he made a lot of money off of it. Anyway, like I was saying, I had a lot of company. My Momma always said you got to put the past behind you before you can move on. 6)

And I think that's what my running was all about. I had run

---

6) 미래를 바라보기 전에 과거를 수용하여라. 즉, 미래로 전진하기 위해서는 아픈 과거를 묻어버리라는 뜻.
 (You must accept the past before you look to the future.)

Episode 7. Put the Past Behind You!

for three years, two months, fourteen days, and sixteen hours.

[*Forrest stops running. The group stops behind him. Forrest stands and looks as the group waits expectantly. Forrest turns and look.*]

YOUNG MAN: Quiet. Quiet, he's gonna say something.
FORREST: I'm pretty tired. I think I'll go home now.
YOUNG MAN: Now what are we supposed to do?
FORREST(V.O.): And just like that, my running days was over. So, I went home to Alabama.

TOPICs to DISCUSS

Read the following review and develop your own idea.

> There is a long and fascinating tradition of the holy fool in spiritual literature. These people follow the dictates of the heart and are often able to effect great works of mercy and compassion. Their brand of selflessness is free of reason's madness and the ego's frivolous grandeur. Holy fools pay no heed to the worldly pursuit of power, status, or financial success. That is why they are usually deemed crazy and forced to live as lonely outsiders. Forrest Gump is an enchanting and creative parable about a contemporary holy fool.
>
> – by Frederic and Mary Ann Brussat

Episode 8

I Pronounce You Man and Wife

I Got a Letter from Jenny

SITUATIONs 1.

WATCH the MOVIE

Warming-up Questions & Listening Practice

1. *What did Forrest get from Jenny?*

   One day, out of the blue clear sky, I got a letter from Jenny.

2. *What did Jenny say in her letter?*

   She was wondering if I could come down to Savannah to see her, and that's what I'm doing here.

3. *How could Jenny reach Forrest?*

   She saw me on TV, running,

4. *How is Forrest supposed to find Jenny's house?*

   I'm supposed to go on the Number Nine bus to Richmond Street and get off and go one block left to 1-9-4-7 Henry Street, Apartment 4.

5. *How far is Jenny's house from the bus stop?*

   Why, you don't need to take a bus. Henry Street is just five or six blocks down that way.

6. *What did the old woman say when Forrest left her?*

   I hope everything works out for you.

Listen to the audio and check!

FORREST(V.O.): One day, out of the blue clear sky, I got a letter from Jenny, wondering if I could come down to Savannah to see her, and that's what I'm doing here. She saw me on TV, running, I'm supposed to go on the Number Nine bus to Richmond Street and get off and go one block left to 1-9-4-7 Henry Street, Apartment 4.

[*The elderly woman looks at the letter.*]

ELDERLY WOMAN: Why, you don't need to take a bus. Henry Street is just five or six blocks down that way.

FORREST: Down that way?

ELDERLY WOMAN: Down that way.

FORREST: It was nice talking' to you.

ELDERLY WOMAN: I hope everything works out for you.

Junior Forrest

SITUATIONs 2

Warming-up Questions & Listening Practice

1. *What did Jenny say when she met Forrest at her front door?*

   Is this your house?
   Yeah, it's messy right now. I just got off work.

2. *What did Jenny keep in a scrapbook?*

   Hey, I kept, I kept a scrapbook of your, of your clippings and everything.

3. *What did Jenny want to apologize for?*

   There. Listen, Forrest. I don't know how to say this. Um, I just, I want to apologize for anything that I ever did to you, 'cause I was messed up for a long time.

Episode 8. I Pronounce You Man and Wife

4. *What did Jenny thank her friend for?*

   Ah, listen, next week my schedule changes, so I'll be able to, but thanks for picking up.

5. *How did Jenny's friend hurry up to go?*

   No problem. Got to go, Jen. I'm double parked.

Listen to the audio and check!

At Jenny's apartment, Jenny opens the door.

JENNY: Hey! Forrest! How you doing?
FORREST: Hi.
JENNY: Come in. Come in.
FORREST: I got your letter.
JENNY: Oh, I was wondering about that.
FORREST: Is this your house?
JENNY: Yeah, it's messy right now. I just got off work.
FORREST: It's nice. You got air conditioning.

[*Forrest hands Jenny the box of chocolates.*]

FORREST: Ah…
JENNY: Thank you.
FORREST: I ate some.

[*Jenny picks up a scrapbook and turns the pages.*]

JENNY: Hey, I kept, I kept a scrapbook of your, of your clippings and everything. There you are. This, I got your running.
FORREST: I ran a long way. For a long time.
JENNY: There. Listen, Forrest. I don't know how to say this. Um, I just, I want to apologize for anything that I ever did to you,

Episode 8. I Pronounce You Man and Wife

	'cause I was messed up [1] for a long time, and… [*There is a knock at the door. Jenny grabs a young boy.*] Hey, you. This is an old friend from Alabama.
LYNN MARIE:	Oh, how do you do?
JENNY:	Ah, listen, next week my schedule changes, so I'll be able to, but thanks for picking up.
LYNN MARIE:	No problem. Got to go, Jen. I'm double parked. [2]
JENNY:	Okay.
LYNN MARIE:	Bye.

TOPICs to DISCUSS

Read the following review and develop your own idea.

> Throughout, Forrest carries a flame for Jenny, a childhood sweetheart who was raised by a sexually abusive father and is doomed to a troubled life. The character's a bit obvious: Jenny is clearly Forrest's shadow—darkness and self-destruction played against his lightness and simplicity. She's more of a script device than a real character, and her long schlep through the '60s—folk music, drugs, protests and bad relationships— feels like a grab bag of movie cliches.

1) 엉망이다.
2) 주차장이 아닌 곳에 남의 차와 이중으로 주차를 해서 빨리 나가봐야 한다는 의미.

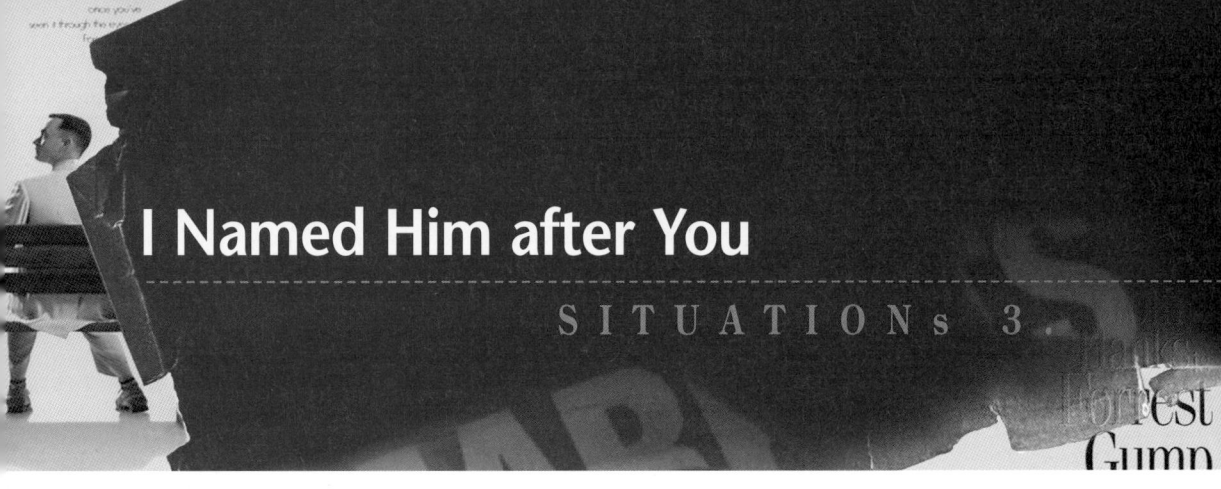

I Named Him after You

SITUATIONs 3

Warming-up Questions & Listening Practice

1. *How does Jenny want her son want to watch TV?*

   Now, can I go watch TV now?
   Yes, you can. Just keep it low.

2. *How did Jenny name her son?*

   I named him after his Daddy.
   He got a daddy named Forrest, too?

3. *What did Jenny say when Forrest looked frightened to find his son?*

   Hey, Forrest, look at me. Look at me, Forrest.
   There's nothing you need to do, okay?
   You didn't do anything wrong. Okay?

Episode 8. I Pronounce You Man and Wife

4. *Why do you think were Forrest frightened?*

   You didn't do anything wrong. Okay?

5. *What did Forrest think of his little son?*

   He's the most beautiful thing I've ever seen. But... is, is he smart, or is he... He's very smart. He's one of the smartest in his class.

6. *What was Forrest Junior doing?*

   "Sesame Street" is on the TV.
   What are you watching?/ Bert and Ernie.

🎧 Listen to the audio and check!

JENNY:	Thanks. This is very good friend, Mr. Gump. Can you say hi to him?
LITTLE BOY:	Hello, Mr. Gump.
FORREST:	Hello.
LITTLE BOY:	Now, can I go watch TV now?
JENNY:	Yes, you can. Just keep it low.
FORREST:	You're a momma, Jenny.
JENNY:	I'm a momma. His name is Forrest.
FORREST:	Like me.
JENNY:	I named him after his Daddy.
FORREST:	He got a daddy named Forrest, too?
JENNY:	You're his daddy, Forrest.
	[Forrest continues to stare at Forrest Jr. Forrest then looks frightened and starts to back away.]
JENNY:	Hey, Forrest, look at me. Look at me, Forrest. There's nothing you need to do, okay? You didn't do anything wrong. Okay? Isn't he beautiful?
FORREST:	He's the most beautiful thing I've ever seen. But… is, is he smart, or is he…
JENNY:	He's very smart. He's one of the smartest in his class.
	Forrest breathes deep. He looks at Jenny, then at Forrest Jr.
JENNY:	Yeah, it's okay. Go talk to him.
	[Forrest walks into the room and sits down next to Forrest Jr. "Sesame Street" is on the TV.]

FORREST: What are you watching.
FORREST: JR. Bert and Ernie.

TOPICs to DISCUSS

> Discuss the father-son relationship in the contemporary society of the United States.

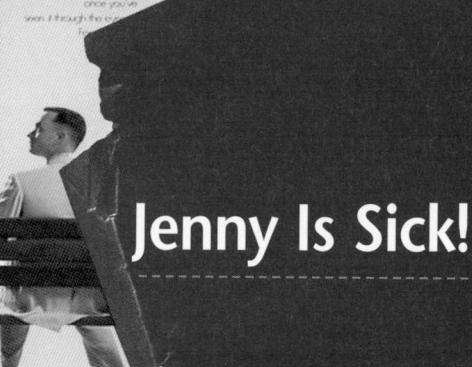

Jenny Is Sick!

SITUATIONs 4

Warming-up Questions & Listening Practice

1. *How is Jenny sick?*

   What, do you have a cough due to cold?

2. *Why can't Jenny get well?*

   I have some kind of virus. And the doctors don't, they don't know what it is. And there isn't anything they can do about it.

3. *What does Forrest suggest to Jenny who is sick?*

   You could come home with me. Jenny, you and little Forrest could come stay at my house in Greenbow. I'll take care of you if you're sick.

4. *How are Lieutanent Dan's new artificial legs made?*

   Yeah, I got new legs. Custom-made titanium alloy.

Episode 8. I Pronounce You Man and Wife

5. *Where is titanium alloy used?*

   It's what they use on the space shuttle.

6. *How is the marriage vow for Forrest and Jenny pronounced?*

   Do you, Forrest, take Jenny to be your wife? Do you, Jenny, take Forrest to be your husband? If so, I pronounce you man and wife.

Listen to the audio and check!

Forrest and Jenny sit on a bench.

JENNY: Forrest, I'm sick.

FORREST: What, do you have a cough due to cold?

JENNY: I have some kind of virus. And the doctors don't, they don't know what it is.³⁾ And there isn't anything they can do about it.

FORREST: You could come home with me. Jenny, you and little Forrest could come stay at my house in Greenbow. I'll take care of you if you're sick.

JENNY: Would you marry me, Forrest?

FORREST: Okay.

[*A group has gathered on the lawn for the wedding.*]

MINISTER: Please take your seats.

LOUISE: Forrest, it's time to start.

JENNY: Hi. Your tie. [*Lt. Dan is walking across the lawn. He uses a cane. A WOMAN is walking next to him.*]

FORREST: Lieutenant Dan? Lieutenant Dan!

LT. DAN: Hello, Forrest.

3) 의사도 그 원인을 규명할 수 없는 바이러스 병에 걸렸다. 1980년대 상황으로 미루어 볼 때 에이즈 병임을 암시한다.

Episode 8. I Pronounce You Man and Wife

FORREST: You got new legs. New legs!
LT. DAN: Yeah, I got new legs. Custom-made titanium alloy.⁴⁾ It's what they use on the space shuttle.
FORREST: Magic legs.
LT. DAN: This is my fiancee, Susan.
FORREST: Lieutenant Dan! [*Susan shakes Forrest's hand.*]
SUSAN: Hi, Forrest.
FORREST: Lieutenant Dan, this is my Jenny.
JENNY: Hey, it's nice to meet you, finally.

[*The group is seated as they watch Forrest and Jenny take vows on the front lawn.*]

MINISTER: Do you, Forrest, take Jenny to be your wife? Do you, Jenny, take Forrest to be your husband? If so, I pronounce you man and wife.

TOPICs to DISCUSS

Read the following review and develop your own idea.

4) I have <u>custom</u> made legs made of <u>titanium alloy</u>: 티타늄 합금으로 특별 제작된 의족.

Episode 9

Dying Is a Part of Life

Scene 1

SITUATIONs 1

Warming-up Questions & Listening Practice

1. *What is Forrest explaining to Jenny?*

   Sometimes it would stop raining long enough for the stars to come out. And then it was nice.

2. *What was the sun-set like?*

   It looks like there were two skies, one on top of the other.

3. *What was the sun-rise like?*

   And then in the desert, when the sun comes up, I couldn't tell where heavens stopped and the earth began. It was so beautiful.

Forrest Gump 영화읽기

Listen to the audio and check!

Understand what they mean and listen to the tape again.

FORREST: Hey.
JENNY: Hey, Forrest, were you scared in Vietnam?
FORREST: Yes. Well, I, I don't know.

Sometimes it would stop raining long enough for the stars to come out.
And then it was nice.
It was like just before the sun goes to bed down on the Bayou.

There was over a million sparkles on
the water, like that mountain lake.
It was so clear, Jenny.
It looks like there were two skies, one on top of the other.

And then in the desert, when the sun comes up,
I couldn't tell where heavens stopped and the earth began.
It was so beautiful.

JENNY:	I wish I could have been there with you.
FORREST:	You were.
JENNY:	I love you.

TOPICs to DISCUSS
Read the following review and develop your own idea.

> The movie is more of a meditation on our times, as seen through the eyes of a man who lacks cynicism and takes things for exactly what they are. Watch him carefully and you will understand why some people are criticized for being "too clever by half." Forrest is clever by just exactly enough.

Scene 2

SITUATIONs 2.

Warming-up Questions & Listening Practice

1. *What happened to Jenny?*

   You died on a Saturday morning.

2. *What did Forrest do with the house of Jenny's father?*

   And I had you placed here under our tree.
   And I had that house of your father's bulldozed to the ground.

3. *What is Mother's philosophy about death?*

   Momma always said dyin' was a part of life. I sure wish it wasn't.

4. *How does Forrest take care of his son?*

   I make sure he combs his hair and brushes his teeth every day.

5. *What did Forrest's son write?*

   He, uh, wrote a letter, and he says I can't read it. I'm not supposed to, so I'll just leave it here for you.
   Jenny, I don't know if Momma was right or if, if it's Lieutenant Dan.

6. *How is Mother's life philosophy different from Lieutenant Dan's?*

   I don't know if we each have a destiny, or if we're all just floating around accidental-like on a breeze but I, I think maybe it's both.

Listen to the audio and check!

You died on a Saturday morning.
And I had you placed here under our tree.
And I had that house of your father's bulldozed to the ground.[1]
Momma always said dyin' was a part of life. I sure wish it wasn't.

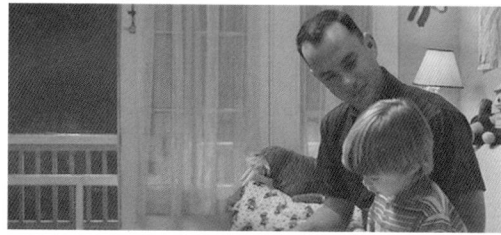

Little Forrest, he's doing just fine.
About to start school again soon.
I make his breakfast, lunch, and dinner every day.
I make sure he combs his hair and brushes his teeth every day.

1) 나는 당신 아버지의 집을 불도저로 밀어버렸소.
2) I don't know if we each have a destiny or if were just floating around accidental-like, on a breeze. "Floating around accidental-like on a breeze" is Forrest's way of expressing a bit of existential philosophy: To float without a particular direction, in a universe not of our making, for no particular reason…

Forrest Gump 영화읽기

Teaching him how to play ping pong.
He's really good. We fish a lot.
And every night, we read a book.
He's so smart, Jenny.
You'd be so proud of him. I am.
He, uh, wrote a letter, and he says I can't read it.
I'm not supposed to, so I'll just leave it here for you.

Jenny, I don't know if Momma was right or if, if it's Lieutenant Dan.
I don't know if we each have a destiny, or if we're all just floating around accidental-like on a breeze but I, I think maybe it's both.[2]
Maybe both is happening at the same time.
I miss you, Jenny. If there's anything you need, I won't be far away.

TOPICs to DISCUSS

Read the following review and develop your own idea.

> Destiny is another concept Gump explores, without ever really resolving what it is. Forrest's Vietnam buddy Bubba (Mykelti Williamson), grievously injured, wonders "Why'd this have to happen?" Dan, raging to Forrest, who rescued him from certain death, cries, "I had a destiny. I was supposed to die in the field with honor." Even Forrest eventually asks his mother (Sally Field), "What's my destiny, Momma?"

Scene 3

SITUATIONs 3

Warming-up Questions & Listening Practice

1. *What is Forrest's son going to do at the class of "Show- and-Tell"?*

   I'm gonna show that for show-and-tell because grandma used to read it to you.

2. *What are you reminded of when you watch the conversation between the bus driver and Forrest's son?*

   You understand this is the bus to school now, don't you?
   Of course, and you're Dorothy Harris and I'm Forrest Gump.

Episode 9. Dying Is a Part of Life

Listen to the audio and check!

[*At the school bus-stop*]

FORREST: Here's your bus Okay.
Hey, I know this.

FORREST JR.: I'm gonna show that for show-and-tell because grandma used to read it to you.[3]

FORREST: My favorite book.
Well, … okay. Hey, there you go.

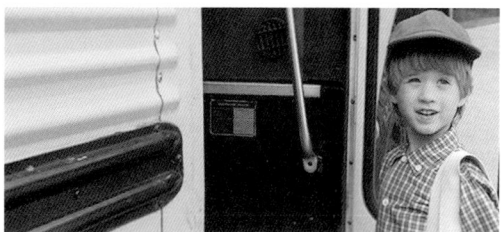

FORREST: Hey, Forrest. Don't… I wanted to tell you I love you.
FORREST JR.: I love you too, Daddy.

3) 미국의 초등학생들이 자기 집안에 있는 유서 깊은 물건들을 학교에 가져가서 그 유래를 설명하는 수업 시간.

FORREST: I'll be right here when you get back.

BUS DRIVER: You understand this is the bus to school now, don't you?
FORREST JR.: Of course, and you're Dorothy Harris and I'm Forrest Gump. [*Forrest Jr. looks over and waves to his father. Forrest nods approvingly.*]

TOPICs to DISCUSS

Destiny Theme In Forrest Gump

The movie Forrest Gump demonstrates the idea of destiny through speech and actions of characters. Three different interpretations of destiny are revealed by three different people. The movie does a good job of using entertainment to appeal to the viewer and incorporate a hidden meaning at the same time. First, Lt. Dan explains his view on what destiny is. Lt. Dan states, "We all have a destiny. Nothing just happens. We all have a plan" This means that every person is set to a particular plan for life when he is born. Each person is locked in to how they will live life and how they will die. Lt. Dan believes he was cheated out of his destiny. He should have died in the war just like his father and grandfathers before him, but Forrest cheated him out of dying. Life after that was very meaningless and non-fulfilling until later in the movie when he changes his views. Lt. Dan's theory of destiny is that people are given a plan in life when they are born into the world. Next, Forrest's mother states her opinion on the idea of destiny. She says, "I believe we make our own destiny."

Appendix

The Commencement Address

— by Steve Jobs

This is the text of the Commencement address by Steve Jobs, CEO of Apple Computer and of Pixar Animation Studios, delivered on June 12, 2005.

I am honored to be with you today at your commencement from one of the finest universities in the world. I never graduated from college. Truth be told, this is the closest I've ever gotten to a college graduation.

세계 최고의 명문으로 꼽히는 이 대학의 졸업식에 여러분과 함께 한 것이 영광입니다. 저는 대학을 졸업하지 못했습니다. 솔직히 말해서, 대학교 졸업식을 이렇게 가까이서 보는 것은 처음이네요.

Today I want to tell you three stories from my life. That's it. No big deal. Just three stories. The first story is about connecting the dots.

오늘, 저는 여러분께 제가 살아오면서 겪었던 세 가지 이야기를 해볼까 합니다. 그게 전부입니다. 별로 대단한 이야기는 아니구요. 꼭 세 가지 이야기 뿐입니다. 먼저, 인생의 전환점에 관한 이야기입니다.

I dropped out of Reed College after the first 6 months, but then stayed around as a drop-in for another 18 months or so before I really quit. So why did I drop out?

전 리드 칼리지에 입학한 지 6개월 만에 자퇴했습니다. 그래도 일년 반 정도는 도강을 듣다, 정말로 그만뒀습니다. 왜 자퇴했을까요?

It started before I was born.
She felt very strongly that I should be adopted by college graduates, so everything was all set for me! It started before I was born. My biological mother was a young, unwed college graduate student, and she decided to put me up for adoption. to be adopted at birth by a lawyer and his wife.

그 것은 제가 태어나기 전까지 거슬러 올라갑니다. 제 생모는 대학원생인 젊은 미혼모였습니다. 그래서 저를 입양보내기로 결심했던 거지요. 그녀는 제 미래를 생각해, 대학 정도는 졸업한 교양있는 사람이 양부모가 되기를 원했습니다. 그래서 저는 태어나자마자 변호사 가정에 입양되기로 되어 있었습니다.

Except that when I popped out they decided at the last minute that they really wanted a girl. So my parents, who were on a waiting list, got a call in the middle of the night asking: "We have an unexpected baby boy; do you want him?"

그들은 여자 아이를 원했던 걸로 알고 있습니다. 그들 대신 대기자 명단에 있던 양부모님들은 한밤중에 걸려온 전화를 받고: "어떡하죠? 예정에 없던 사내아이가 태어났는데, 그래도 입양하실 건가요?"

They said: "Of course."

"물론이죠"

My biological mother later found out that my mother had never graduated from college and that my father had never graduated from high school. She refused to sign the final adoption papers.

그런데 알고보니 양어머니는 대졸자도 아니었고, 양아버지는 고등학교도 졸업 못한 사람이어서 친어머니는 입양동의서 쓰기를 거부했습니다.

She only relented a few months later when my parents promised that I would someday go to college. And 17 years later I did go to college.

친어머니는 양부모님들이 저를 꼭 대학까지 보내주겠다고 약속한 후 몇개월이 지나서야 화가 풀렸습니다. 17년 후, 저는 대학에 입학했습니다.

But I naively chose a college that was almost as expensive as Stanford, and all of my working-class parents' savings were being spent on my college tuition.

그러나 저는 멍청하게도 바로 이곳, 스탠포드의 학비와 맞먹는 값비싼 학교를 선택했습니다. 평범한 노동자였던 부모님이 힘들게 모아뒀던 돈이 모두 제 학비로 들어갔습니다.

After six months, I couldn't see the value in it. I had no idea what I wanted to do with my life and no idea how college was going to help me figure it out.

결국 6개월 후, 저는 대학 공부가 그만한 가치가 없다는 생각을 했습니다. 내가 진정으로 인생에서 원하는 게 무엇인지, 그리고 대학교육이 그것에 얼마나 어떻게 도움이 될지 판단할 수 없었습니다.

And here I was spending all of the money my parents had saved their entire life. So I decided to drop out and trust that it would all work out OK.

게다가 양부모님들이 평생토록 모은 재산이 전부 제 학비로 들어가고 있었습니다. 그래서 모든 것이 다 잘 될거라 믿고 자퇴를 결심했습니다.

It was pretty scary at the time, but looking back it was one of the best decisions I ever made. The minute I dropped out I could stop taking the required classes that didn't interest me, and begin dropping in on the ones that looked interesting.

당시에는 두려웠지만, 뒤돌아 보았을때 제 인생 최고의 결정 중 하나였던 것 같습니다. 자퇴한 순간, 흥미없던 필수과목들을 듣는 것은 그만두고 관심있는 강의만 들을 수 있었습니다.

It wasn't all romantic. I didn't have a dorm room, so I slept on the floor in friends' rooms, I returned coke bottles for the 5¢ deposits to buy food with, and I would walk the 7 miles across town every Sunday night to get one good meal a week at the Hare Krishna temple.

그렇다고 꼭 낭만적인 것만도 아니었습니다. 전 기숙사에 머물 수 없었기 때문에 친구 집 마룻바닥에 자기도 했고 한 병당 5센트씩하는 코카콜라 빈병을 팔아서 먹을 것을 사기도 했습니다. 또 매주 일요일, 단 한번이라도 제대로 된 음식을 먹기 위해 7마일이나 걸어서 하레 크리슈나 사원의 예배에 참석하기도 했습니다.

I loved it. And much of what I stumbled into by following my curiosity and intuition turned out to be priceless later on. Let me give you one example:

맛있더군요. 당시 순전히 호기와 직감만을 믿고 저지른 일들이 후에 정말 값진 경험이 됐습니다. 예를 든다면

Reed College at that time offered perhaps the best calligraphy instruction in the country. Throughout the campus every poster, every label on every drawer, was beautifully hand calligraphed.

그 당시 리드 칼리지는 아마 미국 최고의 서체 교육을 제공했던 것 같습니다. 학교 곳곳에 붙어있는 포스터, 서랍에 붙어있는 상표들은 너무 아름다웠구요.

Because I had dropped out and didn't have to take the normal classes, I decided to take a calligraphy class to learn how to do this.

어차피 자퇴한 상황이라, 정규 과목을 들을 필요가 없었기 때문에 서체에 대해서 배워보기로 마음먹고 서체 수업을 들었습니다.

I learned about serif and san serif typefaces, about varying the amount of space between different letter combinations, about what makes great typography great. It was beautiful, historical, artistically subtle in a way that science can't capture, and I found it fascinating.

그때 저는 세리프와 산세리프체를, 다른 글씨의 조합간의 그 여백의 다양함을, 무엇이 위대한 타이포그래피를 위대하게 만드는지를 배웠습니다. 그것은 '과학적' 인 방식으로는 따라하기 힘든 아름답고, 유서 깊고, 예술적으로 미묘한 것이었

고, 전 매료되었습니다.

None of this had even a hope of any practical application in my life. But ten years later, when we were designing the first Macintosh computer, it all came back to me.

이런 것들 중 어느 하나라도 제 인생에 실질적인 도움이 될 것 같지는 않았습니다. 그러나 10년 후 우리가 첫번째 매킨토시를 구상할 때, 그 것들은 고스란히 빛을 발했습니다.

And we designed it all into the Mac. It was the first computer with beautiful typography. If I had never dropped in on that single course in college, the Mac would have never had multiple typefaces or proportionally spaced fonts. And since Windows just copied the Mac, it's likely that no personal computer would have them.

우리가 설계한 매킨토시에 그 기능을 모두 집어넣었으니까요. 그것은 아름다운 서체를 가진 최초의 컴퓨터였습니다. 만약 제가 그 서체 수업을 듣지 않았다면 매킨토시의 복수서체 기능이나 자동 자간 맞춤 기능은 없었을 것이고 맥을 따라한 윈도우도 그런 기능이 없었을 것이고, 결국 개인용 컴퓨터에는 이런 기능이 탑재될 수 없었을 겁니다.

If I had never dropped out, I would have never dropped in on this calligraphy class, and personal computers might not have the wonderful typography that they do.

만약 학교를 자퇴하지 않았다면, 서체 수업을 듣지 못했을 것이고 결국 개인용 컴퓨터가 오늘날처럼 뛰어난 글씨체들을 가질 수도 없었을 겁니다.

Of course it was impossible to connect the dots looking forward when I was in college.

물론 제가 대학에 있을 때는 그 순간들이 내 인생의 전환점이라는 것을 알아챌 수 없었습니다.

But it was very, very clear looking backwards ten years later.

그러나 10년이 지난 지금에서야 모든 것이 분명하게 보입니다.

Again, you can't connect the dots looking forward; you can only connect them looking backwards.

달리 말하자면, 지금 여러분은 미래를 알 수 없습니다: 다만 현재와 과거의 사건들만을 연관시켜 볼 수 있을 뿐이죠.

So you have to trust that the dots will somehow connect in your future.

그러므로 여러분들은 현재의 순간들이 미래에 어떤식으로든지 연결된다는 걸 알아야만 합니다.

You have to trust in something—your gut, destiny, life, karma, whatever.

여러분들은 자신의 배짱, 운명, 인생, 카르마(업) 등 무엇이든지 간에 '그 무엇' 에 믿음을 가져야만 합니다.

This approach has never let me down, and it has made all the difference in my life.

이런 믿음이 저를 실망시킨 적이 없습니다. 그리고 그것이 제 인생에서 남들과는 다른 모든 '차이' 들을 만들어냈습니다.

My second story is about love and loss.

두 번째는 사랑과 상실입니다.

I was lucky I found what I loved to do early in life.

저는 운 좋게도 인생에서 정말 하고싶은 일을 일찍 발견했습니다.

Woz and I started Apple in my parents garage when I was 20.

제가 20살 때, 부모님의 차고에서 워즈(스티브 워즈니악)와 함께 애플의 역사가 시작됐습니다.

We worked hard, and in 10 years Apple had grown from just the two of us in a garage into a $2 billion company with over 4000 employees.

우리는 열심히 일해서, 차고에서 2명으로 시작한 애플은 10년 후에 4000명의 종업원을 거느린 2백억 달러짜리 기업이 되었습니다.

We had just released our finest creation—the Macintosh—a year earlier, and I had just turned 30. And then I got fired.

제 나이 29살, 우리는 최고의 작품인 매킨토시를 출시했습니다. 그러나 이듬해 저는 해고당했습니다.

How can you get fired from a company you started?

내가 세운 회사에서 내가 해고 당하다니!

Well, as Apple grew we hired someone who I thought was very talented to run the company with me,

당시, 애플이 점점 성장하면서, 저는 저와 함께 회사를 경영할 유능한 경영자를 데려와야겠다고 생각했습니다.

and for the first year or so things went well.

> 처음 1년정도는 그런대로 잘 돌아갔습니다.

But then our visions of the future began to diverge and eventually we had a falling out.

> 그런데 언젠가부터 우리의 비전은 서로 어긋나기 시작했고, 결국 우리 둘의 사이도 어긋나기 시작했습니다.

When we did, our Board of Directors sided with him. So at 30 I was out. And very publicly out.

> 이 때, 우리 회사의 경영진들은 존 스컬리의 편을 들었고, 저는 30살에 쫓겨나야만 했습니다. 그것도 아주 공공연하게.

What had been the focus of my entire adult life was gone, and it was devastating.

> 저는 인생의 초점을 잃어버렸고, 뭐라 말할 수 없는 참담한 심정이었습니다.

I really didn't know what to do for a few months.

> 전 정말 말 그대로, 몇 개월 동안 아무 것도 할 수가 없었답니다.

I felt that I had let the previous generation of entrepreneurs down - that I had dropped the baton as it was being passed to me.

> 마치 달리기 계주에서 바톤을 놓친 선수처럼, 선배 벤처기업인들에게 송구스런 마음이 들었고

I met with David Packard and Bob Noyce and tried to apologize for screwing up so badly.

> 데이비드 패커드(HP의 공동 창업자)와 밥 노이스(인텔 공동 창업자)를 만나 이렇게 실패한 것에 대해 사과하려했습니다.

I was a very public failure, and I even thought about running away from the valley.

> 저는 완전히 '공공의 실패작' 으로 전락했고, 실리콘 밸리에서 도망치고 싶었습니다.

But something slowly began to dawn on me.

> 그러나 제 맘 속에는 뭔가가 천천히 다시 일어나기 시작했습니다.

I still loved what I did. The turn of events at Apple had not changed that one bit.

> 전 여전히 제가 했던 일을 사랑했고, 애플에서 겪었던 일들조차도 그런 마음들을 꺾지 못했습니다.

I had been rejected, but I was still in love. And so I decided to start over.
전 해고당했지만, 여전히 일에 대한 사랑은 식지 않았습니다. 그래서 전 다시 시작하기로 결심했습니다.

I didn't see it then, but it turned out that getting fired from Apple was the best thing that could have ever happened to me.
당시에는 몰랐지만, 애플에서 해고당한 것은 제 인생 최고의 사건임을 깨닫게 됐습니다.

The heaviness of being successful was replaced by the lightness of being a beginner again, less sure about everything.
그 사건으로 인해 저는 성공이란 중압감에서 벗어나서 초심자의 마음으로 돌아가

It freed me to enter one of the most creative periods of my life.
자유를 만끽하며, 내 인생의 최고의 창의력을 발휘하는 시기로 갈 수 있게 됐습니다.

During the next five years, I started a company named NeXT, another company named Pixar,and fell in love with an amazing woman who would become my wife.
이후 5년 동안 저는 '넥스트', '픽사' 를 만들고, 그리고 지금 제 아내가 되어준 그녀와 사랑에 빠져버렸습니다.

Pixar went on to create the worlds first computer animated feature film, Toy Story, and is now the most successful animation studio in the world.
픽사는 세계 최초의 3D 애니메이션 토이 스토리를 시작으로, 지금은 가장 성공한 애니메이션 제작사가 되었습니다.

In a remarkable turn of events, Apple bought NeXT, I retuned to Apple, and the technology we developed at NeXT is at the heart of Apple's current renaissance.
세기의 사건으로 평가되는 애플의 넥스트 인수와 저의 애플로 복귀 후, 넥스트 시절 개발했던 기술들은 현재 애플의 르네상스의 중추적인 역할을 하고 있습니다.

And Laurene and I have a wonderful family together.
또한 로렌과 저는 행복한 가정을 꾸리고 있습니다.

I'm pretty sure none of this would have happened if I hadn't been fired from Apple.
애플에서 해고당하지 않았다면, 이런 기쁜 일들 중 어떤 한 가지도 겪을 수도 없었을 것입니다

It was awful tasting medicine, but I guess the patient needed it.

정말 독하고 쓰디 쓴 약이었지만, 이게 필요한 환자도 있는가 봅니다.

Sometimes life hits you in the head with a brick. Don't lose faith.

때로 인생이 당신의 뒤통수를 때리더라도, 결코 믿음을 잃지 마십시오.

I'm convinced that the only thing that kept me going was that I loved what I did.

전 반드시 인생에서 해야 할, 제가 사랑하는 일이 있었기에, 반드시 이겨낸다고 확신했습니다.

You've got to find what you love. And that is as true for your work as it is for your lovers.

당신이 사랑하는 것을 찾아보세요. 사랑하는 사람이 내게 먼저 다가오지 않듯, 일도 그런 것이죠.

Your work is going to fill a large part of your life,

'노동' 은 인생의 대부분을 차지합니다.

and the only way to be truly satisfied is to do what you believe is great work.

그런 거대한 시간 속에서 진정한 기쁨을 누릴 수 있는 방법은 스스로가 위대한 일을 한다고 자부하는 것입니다.

And the only way to do great work is to love what you do.

자신의 일을 위대하다고 자부할 수 있을 때는, 사랑하는 일을 하고있는 그 순간 뿐입니다.

If you haven't found it yet, keep looking. Don't settle. As with all matters of the heart, you'll know when you find it.

지금도 찾지 못했거나, 잘 모르겠다해도 주저앉지 말고 포기하지 마세요. 전심을 다한다면 반드시 찾을 수 있습니다.

And, like any great relationship, it just gets better and better as the years roll on.

일단 한번 찾아낸다면, 서로 사랑하는 연인들처럼 시간이 가면 갈수록 더욱 더 깊어질 것입니다.

So keep looking until you find it. Don't settle.

그러니 그 것들을 찾아낼 때까지 포기하지 마세요. 현실에 주저앉지 마세요

My third story is about death.

세 번째는 죽음에 관한 것입니다.

When I was 17, I read a quote that went something like:

17살 때, 이런 경구를 읽은 적이 있습니다.

"If you live each day as if it was your last, someday you'll most certainly be right."

하루 하루를 인생의 마지막 날처럼 산다면, 언젠가는 바른 길에 서 있을 것이다.

It made an impression on me, and since then, for the past 33 years!,

이 글에 감명받은 저는 그 후 50살이 되도록

I have looked in the mirror every morning and asked myself:

매일 아침 거울을 보면서 자신에게 묻곤 했습니다.

"If today were the last day of my life, would I want to do what I am about to do today?"

오늘이 내 인생의 마지막 날이라면, 지금 하려고 하는 일을 할 것인가?

And whenever the answer has been "No" for too many days in a row, I know I need to change something.

아니오! 라는 답이 계속 나온다면, 다른 것을 해야 한다는 걸 깨달았습니다.

Remembering that I'll be dead soon is the most important tool I've ever encountered to help me make the big choices in life.

인생의 중요한 순간마다 '곧 죽을지도 모른다' 는 사실을 명심하는 것이 저에게는 가장 중요한 도구가 됩니다.

Because almost everything?

왜냐구요?

all external expectations, all pride, all fear of embarrassment or failure—

외부의 기대, 각종 자부심과 자만심. 수치스러움와 실패에 대한 두려움들은

these things just fall away in the face of death, leaving only what is truly important.

'죽음' 을 직면해서는 모두 떨어져나가고, 오직 진실로 중요한 것들만이 남기 때문입니다.

Remembering that you are going to die is the best way I know to avoid the trap of thinking you have something to lose.

죽음을 생각하는 것은 무엇을 잃을지도 모른다는 두려움에서 벗어나는 최고의 길입니다.

You are already naked. There is no reason not to follow your heart.

여러분들이 지금 모두 잃어버린 상태라면, 더이상 잃을 것도 없기에 본능에 충실할 수밖에 없습니다.

About a year ago I was diagnosed with cancer.

저는 1년 전쯤 암진단을 받았습니다.

I had a scan at 7:30 in the morning, and it clearly showed a tumor on my pancreas.

아침 7시 반에 검사를 받았는데, 이미 췌장에 종양이 있었습니다.

I didn't even know what a pancreas was.

그전까지는 췌장이란 게 뭔지도 몰랐는데요.

The doctors told me this was almost certainly a type of cancer that is incurable, and that I should expect to live no longer than three to six months.

의사들은 길어야 3개월에서 6개월이라고 말했습니다.

My doctor advised me to go home and get my affairs in order, which is doctor's code for prepare to die.

주치의는 집으로 돌아가 신변정리를 하라고 했습니다. 죽음을 준비하라는 뜻이었죠.

It means to try to tell your kids everything you thought you'd have the next 10 years to tell them in just a few months.

그 것은 내 아이들에게 10년동안 해줄 수 있는 것을 단 몇달 안에 다 해치워야 된단 말이었고

It means to make sure everything is buttoned up so that it will be as easy as possible

for your family.
: 임종시에 사람들이 받을 충격이 덜하도록 매사를 정리하란 말이었고

It means to say your goodbyes.
: 작별인사를 준비하라는 말이었습니다.

I lived with that diagnosis all day.
: 전 불치병 판정을 받았습니다.

Later that evening I had a biopsy, where they stuck an endoscope down my throat, through my stomach and into my intestines, put a needle into my pancreas and got a few cells from the tumor.
: 그 날 저녁 위장을 지나 장까지 내시경을 넣어서 암세포를 채취해 조직검사를 받았습니다.

I was sedated, but my wife, who was there, told me that when they viewed the cells under a microscope
: 저는 마취상태였는데, 후에 아내가 말해주길, 현미경으로 세포를 분석한 결과

the doctors started crying because it turned out to be a very rare form of pancreatic cancer that is curable with surgery.
: 치료가 가능한 아주 희귀한 췌장암으로써, 의사들까지도 기뻐서 눈물을 글썽였다고 합니다.

I had the surgery and thankfully I'm fine now.
: 저는 수술을 받았고, 지금은 괜찮습니다.

This was the closest I've been to facing death, and I hope its the closest I get for a few more decades.
: 그 때만큼 제가 죽음에 가까이 가본 적은 없는 것 같습니다. 또한 앞으로도 수십 년간은 그렇게 가까이 가고 싶지 않습니다.

Having lived through it, I can now say this to you with a bit more certainty than when death was a useful but purely intellectual concept:
: 이런 경험을 해보니, '죽음' 이 때론 유용하단 것을 머리로만 알고 있을 때보다 더 정확하게 말할 수 있습니다.

No one wants to die. Even people who want to go to heaven don't want to die to get there.

아무도 죽길 원하지 않습니다. 천국에 가고 싶다는 사람들조차도 그곳에 가기 위해 죽고 싶어하지는 않죠.

And yet death is the destination we all share. No one has ever escaped it.

그리고 여전히 죽음은 우리 모두의 숙명입니다. 아무도 피할 수 없죠.

And that is as it should be, because Death is very likely the single best invention of Life.

그리고 그래야만 합니다. 왜냐하면 삶이 만든 최고의 발명이 '죽음' 이니까요.

It is Life's change agent. It clears out the old to make way for the new.

죽음은 '인생들' 을 변화시킵니다. 죽음은 새로운 것이 헌 것을 대체할 수 있도록 만들어줍니다.

Right now the new is you, but someday not too long from now, you will gradually become the old and be cleared away.

지금의 여러분들은 그 중에 '새로움' 이란 자리에 서 있습니다. 그러나 언젠가 머지않은 때에 여러분들도 새로운 세대들에게 그 자리를 물려줘야 할 것입니다.

Sorry to be so dramatic, but it is quite true.

너무 극적으로 들렸다면 죄송하지만, 사실이 그렇습니다.

Your time is limited, so don't waste it living someone else's life.

여러분들의 삶은 제한되어 있습니다. 그러니 낭비하지 마십쇼.

Don't be trapped by dogma—which is living with the results of other people's thinking.

도그마—다른 사람들의 생각—에 얽매이지 마십쇼

Don't let the noise of other's opinions drown out your own inner voice.

타인의 소리들이 여러분들 내면의 진정한 목소리를 방해하지 못하게 하세요

And most important, have the courage to follow your heart and intuition.

그리고 가장 중요한 것은 마음과 영감을 따르는 용기를 가지는 것입니다.

They somehow already know what you truly want to become. Everything else is secondary.

이미 마음과 영감은 당신이 진짜로 무엇을 원하는지 알고 있습니다. 나머지 것들은 부차적인 것이죠.

When I was young, there was an amazing publication called The Whole Earth Catalog, which was one of the bibles of my generation.

제가 어릴 때, 제 나이 또래라면 다 알만한 '지구 백과' 란 책이 있었습니다.

It was created by a fellow named Stewart Brand not far from here in Menlo Park, and he brought it to life with his poetic touch.

여기서 그리 멀지 않은 먼로 파크에 사는 스튜어트 브랜드란 사람이 쓴 책인데, 자신의 모든 걸 불어넣은 책이었지요.

This was in the late 1960's, before personal computers and desktop publishing, so it was all made with typewriters, scissors, and polaroid cameras.

PC나 전자출판이 존재하기 전인 1960년대 후반이었기 때문에, 타자기, 가위, 폴라로이드로 그 책을 만들었습니다.

It was sort of like Google in paperback form, 35 years before Google came along:

35년 전의 책으로 된 구글이라고나 할까요.

it was idealistic, and overflowing with neat tools and great notions.

그 책은 위대한 의지와 아주 간단한 도구만으로 만들어진 역작이었습니다.

Stewart and his team put out several issues of The Whole Earth Catalog, and then when it had run its course, they put out a final issue.

스튜어트와 친구들은 몇 번의 개정판을 내놓았고, 수명이 다할 때쯤엔 최종판을 내놓았습니다.

It was the mid-1970s, and I was your age.

그 때가 70년대 중반, 제가 여러분 나이 때였죠.

On the back cover of their final issue was a photograph of an early morning country road,

최종판의 뒤쪽 표지에는 이른 아침 시골길 사진이 있었는데,

Forrest Gump 영화읽기

the kind you might find yourself hitchhiking on if you were so adventurous.

아마 모험을 좋아하는 사람이라면 히치하이킹을 하고 싶다는 생각이 들 정도였지요.

Beneath it were the words: "Stay Hungry. Stay Foolish."

그 사진 밑에는 이런 말이 있었습니다: 배고픔과 함께, 미련함과 함께

It was their farewell message as they signed off. Stay Hungry. Stay Foolish.

배고픔과 함께, 미련함과 함께. 그 것이 그들의 마지막 작별인사였습니다.

And I have always wished that for myself. And now, as you graduate to begin anew, I wish that for you.

저는 이제 새로운 시작을 앞둔 여러분들이 여러분의 분야에서 이런 방법으로 가길 원합니다.

Stay Hungry. Stay Foolish.

배고픔과 함께, 미련함과 함께

Thank you all very much.

감사합니다.